3 —

D1525464

"MOM'S GUIDE" PARENTING YOUR TEENAGE DAUGHTER

BUILD A BETTER CONNECTION WITH YOUR TEEN
GIRL TACKLING ANXIETY, INTENSE EMOTIONS,
DEPRESSION, SELF-ESTEEM ISSUES AND MORE

TAMMY COBBS

CONTENTS

A SPECIAL GIFT TO OUR READERS

Included with your purchase of this book is our *"4 Ways to spend Quality time with your teenage daughter"*.
This checklist will provide you ways to re-connect with your daughter.

Go to the link below and let us know which email address to deliver it to:

www.TammyCobbs.com

INTRODUCTION

When my twins were five years old, we went on a family bus trip to Grand Canyon National Park. A mother and her two teenage daughters were on the seat in front of us in the game vehicle. Even today, 15 years later, I remember the moment. Both mother and daughters seemed so peaceful in each other's company. She had her arms around them, and each time they saw something exciting, they'd lean in to include her. I remember kissing the top of my girls' heads and making a silent vow we would remain as close.

Ten years later, when they were 15, hugging a cactus would have been more affectionate than my twins. The thought of a hug or kiss was more like the proverbial carrot hung in front of me, which I'd never reach. They left dirty clothes and cups in their room, and shoes had long forgotten what the inside of a cupboard looked like. They would humiliate me at every opportunity, and I was a constant source of embarrassment. They'd sneak food out the fridge half an hour before dinner then tell me they were not hungry when dinner was ready. I had no idea if they ever slept, as they were forever tired, except when it came to being with friends —when then they displayed bountiful energy. Their minds changed faster than a high-speed car chase, and their phones were a fancy 21st-century appendage. When I thought I was funny, eyes were rolling in my direction as clearly, I wasn't. And just when I thought I'd gained control of the chaos around me, I'd be reminded I would never have order again.

When teens start biting your head off from a simple "how was school today?" you'll begin believing why teenagers get such a bad rap. No matter the age of your children, as a parent, you're wired to protect them. Holding on to harmony in the household means understanding they're wired to do something too. And it's not to remain under your wings their entire life. Teenagers are evolutionarily triggered to move away from the protection you provide. For them, it's an easy process as their body is programmed to do so. Unfortunately, we have no cut-off age of our protective hold, which is why for parents it's hard to let go.

Hit the rewind button and remember the sleep-deprived days when your children were babies. You lived through 3 am feeding sessions, temper tantrums that turned your cheeks crimson when they wouldn't listen to "no" while you were shopping. You remember, don't you? Those moments you longed for the invention of teleportation, as your head hung in shame as other parents looked at you disapprovingly. You dealt with their boredom during holidays and dramas with friends. The journey has already been long. Yet you enjoyed every rollercoaster ride as you loved them. Press play, and here you are, looking at your children morphing into teenage monsters . . . and you trembling in fear. Well, I can certainly not blame you.

Parenting teenagers means taking on the ethos that long-term outcomes outrank short-term control. Even if you've laid down strong foundations in their youth, there is no guarantee you'll make it through unscathed. Likely, if you have a positive relationship with your children as they move into those years, they'll consider your influence and guidance, but in their own sweet time.

Children need you to lead the way. Teenagers don't need you to lead, they need you by their side.

During adolescence, the brain's frontal lobes where the highest cognitive and emotional networks are formed, mature and strengthen. The adolescent's attention span increases, as does the ability to process information. It can make them angry and frustrated and their strong and astute emotions along with impulsive decisions become dominant nature in this teenage monster that resembles your daughter.

You may assume they have a cushy lifestyle, but behind the scenes, they feel intense pressure. They worry about friends, how they look, their social status, and what the outside world looking in sees and thinks of them. Hopes for a future are forming, of a possible world where they make their own rules. They dream anything is possible and desire love and affection for who they are—even though they haven't figured that one out yet. It's also the time they are more likely to experiment with every parent's dreaded fears; sex, drugs, and alcohol.

The struggle for parents to remain distant can be a risky yet delicate process as you don't love them any less. Yet when your teenager's time is dominated by staying out late, keeping bad company, engaging in precarious behavior, listening to music that makes you cringe, and dressing inappropriately, you can't help but wonder if all these twists and turns that shape their lives are necessary.

A common thread between teenagers is that they're changing, forming new identities, beliefs and opinions that allow them to make decisions independently and ultimately, set themselves up to be your equal. They want you to notice and respect them as intelligent and mature people. The way they go about it, though, can be mind-boggling especially when they withdraw themselves into solitary cocoons. At that moment, many parents give in and ignore them, figuring perhaps that's the only option. Sadly, this can become a negative pattern as ignoring their behavior is one thing, but ignoring the person is another.

Our teenagers see us as controlling, we see them as childish and irresponsible, yet they're quite happy to play the "I'm not a child anymore" card when it suits them. And if you stop to think about it, that's exactly the point. Teenagers are the connective tissue that links adulthood to childhood. They are between both worlds. When we hold onto those reigns too tight and for too long, inevitably, conflict follows. The worst mistake we can make is presuming that they don't need us anymore, even when they give us their icy cold glare. They do, but in a different way than they did before.

Connection lies in listening to them and their perspectives. We need to assume the same child we love is inside and their intentions are good. We can learn to accept clashes in values when we open our eyes to how amazing our teenagers are; the way they grow, as do their opinions and ideas. You can almost see their cognitive development changing gears before you and it's exciting. Looking beyond the drama, they have hope and optimism of a future they create for themselves, and you want to be the one believing in them every step of the way.

If you could have a home with your teenagers where their jovial energy bounds in and out, even when that energy seems explosive, you'd do it as their enthusiasm for life is catching. They have more fun, drama, awkward moments, and mistakes than they know what to do with, and they love every part of it. As parents, it's useful to remember that our own behavior can improve or worsen the situation. We need to be good role models and open our hearts to how amazing they are, and how much we long to be part of it.

Fifteen years later, and my daughters are now 20 years old. I've come to realize the world they move into is already geared to knock them down at every opportunity despite their passion to jump into life as an adult. I've learned that connecting with your teens in the moment, without worrying about the past or future, is where the door to empathy and compassion opens opportunities for growth.

Life as a parent hasn't always been easy, but along the way, I've learned the most amazing things about my children and myself. As a mother of twin girls, I also have other children; twin boys. Common sense would have dictated that I spend four years at university to understand the psychology of teens, but I took the hands-on approach and had four children instead.

Born in London, England my parents moved to Toronto, Canada when I was 10 years old. As a child, I had a curious nature and I've always believed knowledge is there to be shared. As my children went through their teenage years, I cannot express how much faith I lost in myself as everything I thought I had fought hard for—family connections—crumbled around me. If I had known some of the things I do now, I would have approached those teenage years differently.

What is it like raising teenage girls?

I'm not sure I'm at liberty to use the words that would truly express my thoughts on the matter, because in truth I think I aged fifteen years while they only aged five. Let's face it, being a parent of teenagers is a relentless onslaught of emotions, perpetual feelings of inadequacy, frustration and desperation and you can't help but be overwhelmed with the complexity of . . . how do I get through it?

I suggest you pour yourself a cup of tea, grab a pen and paper while I unravel the world of teenage daughters. I learned there is genuinely a way for us to grow as human beings at the same time as our teenage children.

For it to happen, both child and parent need to be part of the same process.

A Quick Lesson in History

The word adolescent originates from a Latin word meaning "growing up." The expectations and requirements of teenagers haven't always been the same throughout history. Between the 5th and 15th centuries, there was no such thing as adolescence. Our human rite of passage was more tied in with our primal ancestors. You were born, your parents cared and nurtured you, and when you could survive on your own, you did. Parents fulfilled their responsibility to get you on your feet and what life did to you thereafter was your affair. While humankind progressed somewhat into the 16th and 17th centuries, parents still believed that showing affection and "fussing" led to poorly behaved children.

Heading into the 18th and 19th centuries, parents began to understand how important nurturing and education could be to the future of their children. Education through the church became the norm—well, for richer families anyway. For the poor, it was an unnecessary luxury as if they were capable of working, they contributed to the family. Throughout the Industrial Revolution, the work of children in factories was paramount. After the Industrial Age is where the teenagers we know today began to develop.

In the 20th and 21st centuries, we came to understand that there were challenges teenagers faced that differed from adults. For a large part, there was no proof—just theories based on observation. Today, we've come to understand a great deal more as we decipher the complexities of the human brain. Many teenagers go through these years positively, enthusiastically, and committed. They don't become isolated, depressed, or turn to substance abuse, and they don't disrespect family and school peers. Modern understanding has allowed us to realize changes are also instigated from biological, social, cultural, and economic influences, and every teenager will experience life during these years differently.

In the past decade alone, the lives of teens have changed with the infiltration of technology and social media. How they learn and interact with each other differs from the generations before them. Every generation is molded in some way through the events of the world around them. And every individual is molded and influenced by their direct surroundings.

ENTERING ADOLESCENCE

Ah, the sweet tweens! That preadolescent time in your daughter's life where she enters her teenage years. Your little angel with bouncing pigtails in her hair begins to fade to oblivion as puberty begins to set in. It's as though she just leaped off the diving board. The ground she left behind was her stable childhood. Now she's airborne, and the time ahead is unknown until she touches the water into adulthood. She needs you now more than ever as her emotions heighten, and moods become unpredictable. In these times conflict can sadly come too easily. She becomes more reflective internally and conscious about herself and her place in this ever-changing world. She'll begin to worry about how she looks and how she's perceived by other people. What happens during these "tween" years, is that what we as parents see on the surface is the tip of the iceberg compared to what is going on internally. She begins to allow her friends to take precedence in her life and she'll want to start pushing the rules like never before. Perhaps she used to enjoy modeling clay and now it's "for babies."

It may seem as if her interests are all over the place. Once, the idea of Cinderella's glass slipper being the perfect fit was enough for her. Now, she needs to try on every shoe in the shop to find which one speaks her language. She's on the hunt for the "right fit." She'll begin stressing over what you may think are little things as her hormones fluctuate.

During these preteen years, the development of your daughter's brain makes it understandable why one day she'll come across as mature, and the next, you feel like you have a six-year-old on your hands. Her brain is undergoing critical development between the prefrontal cortex and the emotion centers in the back of the brain. The prefrontal cortex is the decision-making part of the brain and allows us to plan, solve problems, control impulses, and understand that our actions have consequences. This cortex is only fully developed in a person's twenties, so in the early stages of development, it's very weak. This means that your child is subconsciously swapping between the back and front cortexes, leaving her vulnerable and incredibly indecisive. And believe me, this confusion frustrating them as much as you, causes the brain to revert to utilizing the amygdala to make decisions and solve problems. Given the amygdala is a part of the brain associated with emotions and aggression, it's easy to see that they come to the forefront and not necessarily because they all of a sudden think you're a horrible person.

Let's face it, that's certainly the way they make us as parents feel. While your daughter may avidly tell you otherwise, you're as integral now as you were when she was a toddler. How you guide her in these years will either help build a healthy brain or make it harder for both her and you, in the long run. It's a time when separation-individuation occurs. This is when your daughter is trying to separate herself from you and attempt to figure out who she is as a person and where she fits into the world. She's searching for her identity that is not regulated by childish thoughts and ideals. She'll begin culminating her own values and morals and question your ideals and morals to monitor and figure out her own.

She will begin analyzing things more logically as well as abstractly and that not all things are necessarily equal or simple. She will also start seeing things from other perspectives as well as looking towards her own future. Helping her to strengthen the prefrontal cortex during this time allows her to grow and mature so that she doesn't feel as if she's freefalling until she hits the water.

Take Action

Given she's starting to think about her future, make her understand that her actions influence the present and the future. Talk openly about consequences when it comes to actions. When you talk to her about these things, don't talk as if she's a child. While she may not be an adult, she has a strong desire to feel respected by you so give her validation that she is clever enough to understand what you're saying. When she was little, you spoke age-appropriate conversations to her. You still need to, but not in the same manner as before. Parenting today doesn't end when children are 15 or 17, we're all aware of that. We assist our children in understanding complex challenges. What relationship you had before the teenage years is not an indicator to their transition, but it will impact the experience for both of you. Many teenagers agree that their behavior is influenced by how they were brought up. So, it's never too late!

While many of us are no experts on reading body language, we naturally understand the basic tools. But children don't. Reading other people's emotions is a skill that becomes more developed as we mature. The best way to teach your daughter this is by acknowledging your own feelings and actions. Through you, she'll understand body language and the true meanings of emotions. When my girls were going through their tween years, I didn't always think they would understand the background between what I had said and what I was feeling, and I would bury my feelings in the process. Their intuitiveness so often amazed me as they began to decipher my subtle traits. It would never take long before one of them would approach me and tell me they knew I didn't mean what I said. They could see it in my face. Life is about balance, so when you do open up about negative feelings like feeling tired or sad, remember to validate happy emotions too. Perhaps your daughter wants your input on picking an outfit. Tell her how happy that makes you feel.

Problem-Solving

A massive change in a teenager's brain is the development of problem-solving skills. Strengthening this skill is a necessity during teenage years and most definitely later in life. Hold yourself back from attempting to fix or correct your daughter's problems. I'm fussy and overly organized. I often wanted to do things for my daughters as I knew I could do it better and quicker.

Looking back, I cannot believe I took that approach as it didn't allow them the space to learn how to resolve problems. If she has a problem, talk her through it. Ask her what different perspectives on the situation might be as well as different solutions and possible outcomes. The more she attempts to solve her problems, the more natural it will become to assess them from a variety of perspectives.

Be a Role Model

While your daughter may be reaching for the stars when it comes to her individuality, she isn't there yet. Being a good role model is the best way to support her emotional and mental growth. As a child, she looked up to you for directions. While it may appear her attempt at doing anything that opposes you is at the forefront; she's always watching and listening to your guidance. Your relationship with her was the first relationship she ever had, and it is that relationship that offers her a template of how to move through life. That template allows her to figure out the difference between positive and negative relationships, what friendship means, and that every relationship requires a mutual amount of communication, understanding, and honesty.

This is just as important when it comes to your feelings, not only your actions. Through you, she'll ascertain how you manage and deal with emotions. Perhaps you came home from a grueling day at work and you're utterly exhausted. The mere thought of dealing with your daughter's drama and having to cook food for the family makes you want to hide yourself in the cupboard. Cupboards are rather dark, and your daughter will think you've gone mad. So, the best solution would be to own up to it. Tell her you're sorry, your day at work has been miserable. You're going to shower, change and wind down a bit and then you'd be happy to talk over her worries. In this way, she sees that it's ok to say that you're not coping or not feeling up to something. It is, however, crucial that you do what you said you would and talk to her afterwards.

Listening

Have you ever been in a position where you haven't told your children certain things, but they know? They are so smart and crafty as they're always listening— even when we think they aren't. If your daughter wants to talk about a topic, it's imperative your focus is on her and you're not listening with half an ear while doing something else. Show that you care about what is happening in her life by offering her 100% of your attention. I'm not saying you have to drop what you're doing but tell her you'll be free in half an hour. Listening means your personal opinion shouldn't be at the forefront.

One of my daughters—and I laugh at the memory— would sometimes get so excited after school. If I was busy, I have been inclined to pick up my phone and do a few things while listening to her. Her response would always be, "Mom! Put that phone down. I need you to listen!" If you listen to your daughter, do you realize what happens? She is prepared to listen in return. It's true. She is more inclined to listen to what you have to say if she believes you are truly listening to her in return. I guarantee her friends do listen to her. By not doing the same, you open the door for her to listen to her friends' guidance above your own.

While you listen, keep your body language in check and don't be shocked by something she confides in you. If it's something she's already done, you cannot change that. Listening means holding back judgment. At least until you have heard the entire story. And even then, if you want her to continue confiding in you, getting angry about something she's done won't strengthen that. As much as you teach her to approach problem-solving from different angles, you need to do the same.

Clothes Are More than Fabric

As your daughter explores her identity, limits, and boundaries, she will also begin exploring new styles of clothing. Perhaps she thinks gothic, anime or steam-punk, for example, are the height of individuality.

Perhaps she keeps veering towards short tops and skirts. When you look at her, you can't understand any of it. Were you any different when you were a teenager? Didn't you want to experiment with clothes because it was fun, and you weren't yet sure what "type" of person you were?

The days of buying her clothes no longer exist. Instead, make a date to take her out shopping, enjoy the time together and allow her to make her choices with your guidance. Ask her what style of clothes she likes as it shows you're interested because you care. When she strays from what you consider acceptable, allow some element of freedom. You may not want her to wear heavy metal clothing, but you need to allow her some scope. Perhaps there are two tops she wants, and you don't like either of the two. Compromise. Pick the better of the two and tell her you'll allow her to have that top, but not the other one. For some parents, that thought may be inconceivable. Consider it this way, if you put down your foot it will cement the thought in her head that while she *thought* you didn't understand, she now *knows* you don't. Which is worse? Wearing a top that has skulls on it or cultivating the divide between the two of you?

As long as your daughter does not harm her character, some freedom to experiment should be allowed. I had a good friend in high school, and especially in her mid to late teens, she often wore short body-fitting dresses. She had the longest legs, and she drew attention. A few years passed and by the time she was 20, she was wearing long hippy-type dresses and was against showing off her body. Nothing happened in her life for her to close herself off, she simply grew up and concluded that what she was wearing didn't highlight and reflect her inner personality. One revealing dress does not indicate a future tainted in promiscuity.

Talk to your daughter about trends and use this opportunity as a lesson. Perhaps her idols wear expensive clothing and accessories. Talk to her about the brands and where those clothes come from. Why are they important to her? What does she think it says about her when she wears them? Teach her all the pros and cons. Perhaps she's set on having a brand name and you know they employ slave labor, so show her a video to educate her. Not that you're denying her, but at least she becomes aware of the consequences of her choices. If she still wants it, try to work out a schedule where she can earn extra money to pay for it herself. Don't shoot down her desires because you don't agree with them.

Perhaps your daughter cares deeply about the world and environment around her and has no interest in the word "fashion." Encourage her to hold on to her belief system and sustainability. Take her to second-hand clothing stores and show her all the clothing available out there that she could wear or tailor-make to her style.

Seductive Social Media Posts

The exploitation of sexual imagery is freely visible on social media as well as advertising campaigns. Constant exposure leads young girls to decide at a very young age what they "should" look like in order to be attractive. Being in the parenting seat my natural instinct is to grab my daughters and put a heavy cloak around them so no male on the planet can see what their body looks like.

In an era of social media, what your daughter wears and posts can give you gray hair before your time. TikTok and other social media are widely popular for young females. Equally popular is the sexual predation that happens on these platforms. Most social media platforms make use of algorithms to supply more in a person's news feed of what they like. Once a predator keeps liking young girls dancing or posing, they will keep being fed those types of videos. It's like feeding cookies to Cookie Monster.

Being impressionable as they are, your daughter may look to other females on social media for validation on what is appealing and appropriate. This often doesn't help your plight any more than retail stores. Sometimes I used to go into retail stores and see clothes for 14-year-olds and I'd think . . . really? Five centimeters shorter and I'd see her underpants! Marketing and brands don't help and racks on racks offering skimpy clothing are found in the most influential fashion stores catering to teenagers. They're not at the age where they understand how negatively adults might view their attire. In all honesty, why would they think anything is wrong when their friends are all wearing the same thing?

If I grew up in a time of phones and selfies, I probably would have posted some photos too. Especially when a high-school boyfriend broke my heart and I'd be posting those "look what you're missing" sexy and happy with friends posts to wreak revenge with my overly active emotions. Wouldn't that be normal as a teenager?

Having a greater perspective always helps and there are many reasons your daughter might be posting provocative images on social media or wearing inappropriate clothing. Unless you bring up the topic, you'll never understand what approach she takes when posting the pictures.

- Perhaps she sees celebrities doing it and doesn't see the difference in her doing it because of her age.
- Perhaps all her friends are doing it, so she follows suit in an effort to fit in.
- Perhaps a person she looks up to at school is doing it.
- Perhaps she's feeling isolated, and this is a means of drawing people to her as she seeks attention.
- Perhaps her changing body makes her uncomfortable and this is how she deals with it.
- Perhaps the images make her feel powerful in her body and make her feel proud.

Setting time limits and monitoring phone usage is definitely the way to go but do it only after you've explored other avenues that address your teenager's feelings and emotions. They seldom understand long-term implications and they need you to establish that boundary line because it could be years till their prefrontal cortex catches up with the rest of their body.

If you find yourself in a position where someone sends you a screenshot of something your daughter posted, don't freak out as if the world is about to end. Laying down any laws of grounding her for months, retracting all her social media accounts, and banning her from using her phone till she finishes school is possibly what you want to do. But it won't get you very far. One of the key elements I learned with my daughters when it came to clothing I didn't approve of, was steering clear of ridiculing and shaming. She is still the daughter you love. Shame instills one thing in her and that is backing away from you as you indicate she is no longer good enough for you. Telling her that her clothing is disgusting doesn't mean she'll have any desire to please you and alter it. It simply affirms her feelings of self-doubt that haunt every teenager.

It's natural for daughters to start feeling and thinking in a more sexual way. Your daughter growing up, so you need to accept it. Make her understand from your experiences what the world is like for women and that sometimes it can feel like a crappy place, and she needs to be in charge of her body. Teach her to be wholesome about her sexuality. This could be by reading age-appropriate romance books or taking your daughter out shopping for bras. Allow her to explore her oncoming sexuality in ways that are not demeaning and don't lose your head in the process.

What is considered appropriate will vary from family to family. Whatever you decide is acceptable is your call. Most important when you talk to her about inappropriate clothing is to not take the approach of shaming. Labeling her clothes as slutty or cheap means she'll take it personally and think she is. As an adult, you understand how provocative clothing can draw the wrong attention, but she doesn't as she's still young and can't understand something from your point of view. Change the way you approach clothing and gain information about why she thinks it's appropriate. That way you'll have a deeper understanding of her perspective.

You're a mother, a woman. You understand that life as a female is at times difficult and fraught with empowerment and objectification issues. We've placarded women's rights for years and the daughters of today stand for female empowerment. Many young women don't see what difference their intelligence, or beauty for that matter, has to do with the clothes they wear.

Boundaries

While you need to allow your daughter some scope, don't forget that you're still the adult and while you don't want them pushing hard against you, you have every right as the parent and adult to continue handing out the required boundaries and consequences while she's living under your roof. Allow her to question them and understand your reasoning rather than "because I said so" which will never work.

Always remember, always—she still needs you! She's unsure of how far she can push the boundaries and you as the parent is there to dictate what they are. She wants your direction, even if she won't admit it. Guide, support, and understand they are trying to fit in with peers. When reinforcing a boundary, she may wonder what the point is, so give your reason why you set the boundary. It will allow her to understand that you have reasons behind what you do and don't make up what she considers pointless rules to make her life difficult.

Hygiene

Teenagers aren't all alike and while one daughter may spend too many hours making herself "perfect" in the bathroom, another teenager needs to be dragged to wash her hair and body more than once a week. During puberty, the body changes and children sweat and smell more than before. Teach your daughter the importance of hygiene. In many ways, they are still children, and may not want to start caring for their body like an adult —especially when puberty hair grows. The body releases different oils and odors through the skin, so using bath soap and hair shampoo is necessary. Get dirty with your explanations; it will only serve to encourage. Find a video or talk about skin bacteria that feed on sweat. It will likely send your daughter running into the shower that evening. Like any conversation with your teenage daughter, don't shame her by telling her she stinks. Instead, tell her you've bought a new fragrant shampoo, for example, and you'd love to see what she thinks.

If your daughter was anything like mine, they had better things to do like chatting with friends than bathing when they were supposed to. One of my daughters was a procrastinator of note. A shower would be pushed from one hour to the next throughout the evening and before she knew it, she'd run out of time, and I was hollering for them to get ready for bed down the hallway. What she was doing was evading responsibility and as with any missed chore or respon- sibility, providing a consequence for her inaction was necessary. There is nothing wrong with telling your daughter not showering for two days isn't healthy. Take her phone and tell her until she sorts herself out, she will not see her phone again. Then lay down some ground rules that if you need to keep reminding her of the importance of hygiene, the time frame she loses her phone will escalate. Choices have consequences and that doesn't change when she's an adult so the sooner she learns that the better.

If your daughter has mental health problems, this can also impact hygiene. Depression tends to give a child a lack of interest and energy to take a shower and look after themselves. On the same token, if a child has been abused in a sexual manner, there is every chance she will avoid being naked and in the shower. These are issues that need to be addressed on a higher level and are discussed in later chapters.

The best way around hygiene is to tackle it like chores in the house. If they don't do chores, you take away privileges as a consequence. They'll push for only so long before they bend as they want their privileges back. And when they do, be positive, not vindictive, and tell her how proud you are that she takes hygiene seriously. Don't be her guiding savior either by constantly reminding her that she needs to shower. Open the door but don't step through it with her. If you remind her every day, she'll rely on you to do just that and fail to be responsible for her own time and actions.

Quite simply, as your daughter moves from a tween to a teen, she is beginning to grow up. She develops her own sense of style and taste, and this may seem like a loss of innocence you're not ready for, but maturing is positive. One day they'll leave home, and you need them to be mature individuals when that happens. The biggest difference between those tweens vs. teen years is that you need to prepare yourself for a whole lot more to come. Tweens are still receptive to parents and their individuality is only beginning to form. Once they are bona fide teenagers, their need for independence is evident, and there goes your little girl with pink ribbons in her hair in the blink of an eye.

If there is one piece of sound advice I can offer as a parent as your daughter moves into her teenage years and beyond, is that failure to engage is as much a betrayal and abandonment as over-engaging. Children grow up. They face adverse danger and make poor choices. Be there for them.

Question:

Which of the following factors is the main culprit for your daughter's aggressive outbursts and mood swings?

1. Social media.
2. Hormones.
3. Friends and influence of peers.
4. The developing brain.

FINDING ACCEPTANCE & FITTING IN

Teenagers strive to discover meaning in the world around them, how to fit into it, and how to do it in a holistic manner. Searching for answers drives their sense of self, develops their behavioral traits, and self-acceptance. Often, the largest driving factor in these years is not only how to fit it, but if they'll fit in. As an adult, we understand that strength arises from our differences because life has taught us that. Most teenagers haven't learned that yet, so they desire collectiveness.

Within this yearning to fit in, your daughter may remodel herself to identify with a group of friends. There are social standards she sees from peers and social media and feels there is a certain standard of perfection she's compelled to meet. Does she look as good as the other girls? Do boys find her attractive and if not, what is wrong with her? Does she hang out with the right crowd? The pressure she has on her shoulders in these years—to fit in, do well at school, be liked by boys and other girls—chips away subconsciously. The desire to be liked can be so consuming that it's easy to forget to like yourself in the process.

As this unfolds, you may feel as if your daughter's moods are closely linked with a pendulum as they sway from one direction to the next. Chances are it isn't anything you've done or she's done, but it's what her friends have done. If things are happening in her friends' lives it will affect her directly. On the same token, if everyone in her group of friends is happy with each other, you can let out a sigh of relief; she'll be happy too. There may be days she feels out of sync with her friends and while this is normal, she'll have a hurricane of a mood as she doesn't want to be out of sync; she wants to be in sync all the time.

Teenage girls can be spiteful and nasty, bringing about jealousy and gossip. Girls who are feeling ostracized from a group of friends or other girls, harbor feelings of worthlessness and insecurity. Where they stand within social groups is how they judge themselves and their value as a whole. By their late teenage years, this feeling dissipates to a degree. They become more comfortable and confident in their own abilities and rely less on popularity. Allow your daughter space for her personality to unfold and find like-minded friends she can trust and care for. It's important not to minimize the impact she feels. You know that things will improve and work out, but for her, it's so overwhelming it doesn't seem possible. Don't counter her by telling her "things aren't that bad," or "but we love you." Consider finding out about any school activities where she may be able to meet other girls in a different social setting for her to regain her confidence.

I remember a group of four girls at school when I was 14 years old. They would swear and wear sunglasses in the school hall and for reasons I never knew, they didn't like me. I was so scared of them. If I saw them ahead in the corridor, I would instantly look downwards so they didn't think I was looking at them. If they caught me looking at them, they would swear and ridicule me as they passed. During this time, another girl moved from interstate to the school. We became good friends. She was loved by all—girls and boys alike as she was street-savvy and sassy. I continued to feel as if I was loved by none. Those four girls liked her and during that time, they would look at me, but no longer talk to me. I was desperate to be liked by them, or at least, less hated–which is ironic, as nothing they stood for was of any interest to me. I knew they were people I would never be able to relate to, yet my desire to be liked was above all reasoning.

As our daughters grow their identities are shaped through relationships. You cannot decide what friends they have, but you can decide what relationships are like at home. If you constantly make your daughter feel unworthy and incapable, that is exactly what she will come to believe. If you uplift her and instills confidence in her, she will have it. In many ways, our identity is born out of what other people believe we are. In your daughter's younger years, your eyes were the mirror in which she saw herself. As a teenager, outside factors begin to influence how she sees herself.

The Power of Friendship

Social awareness and power for teens come down to friendships. It can feel overwhelming for parents as suddenly you've lost control. Yet there is validity in a peer group, and your daughter will find it a necessary journey in her self-discovery and begin to distance herself from you. Between the ages of 10 and 15, when your daughter realizes an entire world exists beyond the family, is when fitting in emerges with a vengeance. Peers divide and children form cliques. This group has rules about who is deemed good enough, and who isn't. It deems who is worthy of talking to and what is considered appropriate clothing. If your daughter falls out of sync with the cliques' rules, she faces criticism, and no teenager likes to be thought of as different. They strive to feel "normal" within their group to earn their sense of belonging.

Even when that group advocates what your daughter used to believe as wrong—such as smoking or picking on other girls—they'll stand by these friends. The power of a clique can often be riddled with danger, but they overlook all of it in an effort to belong. It's a natural process we have no control over. However, if you feel your daughter is suffering in finding her way, don't ignore her. Perhaps she doesn't want your help, but she still needs your acknowledgment and doesn't wish to be ignored. Besides, having the answer isn't always what your daughter wants. Keep offering her a safe place where she knows she is welcome to share her feelings and that you'll listen with empathy.

Adolescent friendships are filled with pitfalls. Their social life revolves around negotiating cliques, gossip, and power plays. They accept this ongoing noise amongst peers as a means of expressing their anger and feelings in a way that is not permitted more directly. It can be a delicate game of chess and how they maneuver themselves across the playing board in their teenage years, for them, is imperative.

First, your daughter needs to armor herself. To do this, she needs to create, maintain, and communicate her boundaries and beliefs to other girls. By telling herself she's fine, even when receiving the icy cold shoulder of another girl, it hurts less if her armor is strong. She needs to move across the chessboard swiftly. If her movements aren't fluid people will look at her with doubt, as if she doesn't know what she's doing. She'll falter and be left with self-doubt. It's not that she wants to be the Queen of the chessboard, she simply just doesn't want to be a measly pawn.

What also comes into play in teenage years, is that a daughter's ideal of parents doesn't remain the same. Think for a moment of your own childhood. Do you have fonder memories of your primary school teachers than your high school teachers? As a young child, we trust adults to guide us and assume they know way more than we do. Teenagers? Well, we all know they think they know more than us. It's not that they mean to lower your value in their life, they simply learn that everyone is flawed, including you. They begin to realize that while they may strive for perfection, there is no such thing.

Don't take it personally. After all, you're not perfect so why do you wish your children to keep believing you are? What you can do though, is to never stop striving to be the best person and mother you can be. Be sure to practice what you preach, as your daughter is bound to be watching when you don't. Always lead by example; not through endless explanations.

Losing Her Trust

There was a time that your daughter possibly loved fairies, unicorns, and rainbows. Or perhaps she loved reading, building Legos, and computer coding. And in the flick of that magic wand of youth, her innocent childhood evaporated. What did you do wrong that she doesn't appear to trust you anymore? Once you were besties, now you're frenemies.

I remember when my daughters used to eagerly grab my hand when we went to the shops, and I loved the feeling that they turned to me for security and guidance. In their teenage years, they couldn't distance themselves from me enough and would purposely walk ahead or behind me in an effort to "stand alone." Those moments hurt. I desperately wanted to reconnect but felt powerless. It's hard not to allow these moments to affect you but forcing yourself not to take it personally and distance yourself from your feelings is how you survive.

Hold on to one thought only. You have not lost your daughter's trust. Your love, regardless of age, is immeasurable. When you compliment her on something she's done or what she's wearing and she rolls her eyes in reply or shrugs her shoulders as though she couldn't care less, she does. She may appear as though she doesn't care what you say, but she's listening and still needs to know you're not only there for her, but you stand by her. The ground under her feet is in perpetual tremors. She may not want to hold your hand anymore, but she needs to know it's close by should she need it.

For her to know you're watching and understanding, it's important to make an effort to know what is happening in her life. Know her friends, what they do and are experiencing and ask about them. You might not get much of a reply, and don't beat yourself up about that. Don't do something because you expect acknowledgment. She's not six anymore and she doesn't need to reiterate what you've said to give you a receipt of understanding. Know that she is listening, and the message has been received that you care about her friends, which means you care about her. Or ask her how a math test went. Even if you only receive the reply "ok," don't push for more than she's willing to give or you'll make her shut down even further.

Another way for your daughter to know you're there for her is through the subtle way of using old-fashioned notes. I read about this once and I cannot tell you how much I loved doing it. I did it for years for the girls. Once your daughter is in bed and if you know she has a particularly crucial test or is feeling sad over a boy not liking her or fighting with a friend, write a few words on a piece of paper and put it in her pencil case. The following day she'll see the note. The note might say: "Good luck on your test," or "Trust yourself. It will all be ok." Chances are she may read it very briefly, too scared one of her friends will see you're being a typical mom. Chances are if they ask her, she'll screw up the note and roll her eyes and say, "It's nothing." And that's ok. Don't do it because you want her to thank you. I can guarantee you, though, the note will warm her heart.

Keeping Routines

I'm a lover of routines. Life is busy, especially with two sets of twins. In an effort to keep the door of communication open, establish simple routines that don't take up too much of your daughter's time—time she would prefer to instead allocate to her social connections and activities. Food is often the ideal way to hold the door open. Whether it is telling her she's the salad queen and must make salad for dinner each night, or she must clear the table and do the dishes with you—these are short windows of opportunity to talk. This doesn't mean in those times you cleverly probe to get the answers you want about what is going on in her life either. She's not silly. She'll know exactly what you're trying to do. Talk about life, politics, different cultures, animals, anything that is a "normal" conversation for two adults to talk about.

Perhaps after school, your daughter has an activity and there is a half-hour waiting period. Use that half hour to get a coffee, tea, or milkshake together and do it regularly to establish the routine. She'll come to understand that those moments are open platforms. Allow her to understand that the time you spend together is not there for you to judge, direct, or play the mom role. You're there to listen.

The human brain thrives off connections. When we teach our brain or wire it to think a certain way, it will lean into those connections automatically. I have a friend who severely sprained her ankle years ago. For months she was on the mend and in this time her brain made the connection that to lessen the pain, limping was necessary. Six months later she had an operation on the ankle as it never mended properly. Despite regular physio after the successful operation, she found herself still limping. She didn't need to limp anymore, but her months of recovery had wired her that way. It took unwiring her brain and reconnecting it to teach herself that limping was no longer necessary.

In the same way, predictable and consistent routines are how you benefit your daughter. In those teenage years, the developing prefrontal cortex driving her emotions isn't the most stable. It's why structure in her life is critical and structure comes through routine. Routine promotes self-regulation and teaches her to manage herself and be self-reliant. Consider the fact that following a routine generally requires the other person to buy into it. Remember, "because those are the rules under this house" isn't helpful. Talk to your daughter and encourage her input. If she feels she also had a say in a routine, chances are she'll put more of an effort into following through with it. What works best for her, and you, when it comes to morning routines and getting ready for school? What works best when juggling her homework and household chores? Don't give in to every whim but find a mutually beneficial outcome. Never be afraid to readdress the routine. When it's working well, compliment her. When it isn't working, readdress why it's not working and if you need to restructure it, then do so.

Finding acceptance in the teenage world is paramount. Experiences shape them and through experiences, your daughter will discover what she is good at and what challenges her. Everyone learns differently, views the world differently, and matures differently. Getting her through her teenage years is smoother if you find a middle ground of not being overly demanding, yet still encouraging her that she needs to persevere through hard work.

One of my girls is naturally talented when it comes to math. It was as if she never needed to study. I made the mistake, so I discovered, of reinforcing her in the wrong way. I would congratulate her with words such as "you're so smart!" It wasn't long before I realized her math grades were dropping. She started to believe she was smart enough not to study. What I should have been telling her was things like "congratulations on the hard work." In that way, it would have been an incentive to rise to the next math challenge, and the next. Always compliment the *effort* rather than the ability.

Self-Expression & Body Modification

It doesn't really matter what our age is, it's human nature that when we focus too much on our imperfections, we fail to see the beauty within. Society in a teenager's brain is about perfection. It differs for all, but nevertheless, it's perfection. It dictates what your daughter wears to fit in and how she speaks and holds herself. She might starve herself to be thin, dye her hair rainbow colors, deny herself the things she loves, and eventually, lose touch with the person she once believed herself to be. You'll find yourself sitting at the dinner table, looking at your daughter, and seeing an isolated stranger in front of you instead.

Teenagers often wish to get body piercings or tattoos as a way of expressing themselves and seeking independence. They may want to stand out from the crowd or fit into a crowd. They may want to shock other people to draw attention to themselves. All of these situations are normal emotions for them to go through. It may be about having a shared experience with friends or fearing they will not be respected by friends if they don't follow suit. A teenager may also get a body piercing because they feel pressured by a romantic partner.

If you're in a situation where your daughter wants to pierce her body in a place you disagree with, take a moment to be mindful and don't react in the way you'd like to and blatantly tell her she isn't allowed. Don't hand her a silver platter of opportunity to stand up against you. Approach the situation in a non-judgmental manner and discuss the topic with her. Ask her why she wants one and allow her to problem-solve the solution herself. For example, perhaps she wants a nipple ring as her partner has asked her to get one. Ask her questions such as if things didn't work out with her partner, would she still want it? Or you could ask her if her best friend's boyfriend wanted the same things, what would she tell her friend to help her make her decision. It's important to discuss some pros and cons with her, especially if you believe the piercing is related to sexual pleasures. Tell her about how she increases her risk of sexually transmitted infections due to piercing compromising the protective skin layer as well as general infections and wounds.

If it's another area of her body such as the nose, navel, or on the upper part of her ear and she insists she wants it done and you feel no matter what you say, she's going to get it done without you, tell her you'll only agree if you can take her to get it done. Make sure to take her to a reputable body piercer. Tell her that piercing in those areas is susceptible to problems if the cartilage is pierced instead of the soft tissue.

When it comes to piercings and tattoos, listen to your daughter and her viewpoint. Allow her to feel as though you value her opinion, even if you don't agree with it. Once she's validated her thoughts about it, there is no reason you can't express your own. It doesn't matter whether you're for or against the concept, let her know if you have fears about it. If you have negative feelings, express yourself and she will be happier listening to you talk truthfully rather than simply saying no. Try to compromise where possible if you feel sure she'll do it with or without your approval. Perhaps she wants a large tattoo, try to compromise with a smaller one, in a less visible part of the body. Or suggest when she turns 18 that you'll buy it for her birthday.

Hanging with the Wrong Crowd

For mothers, it can be alarming if your daughter has a friend or she's hanging out with less than "parent-approved" friends. We can't pick their friends. This can lead to many sleepless nights as we lay awake worrying when she's out with people we fear are drinking or abusing substances. Criticizing her friends will leave you with replies such as "you don't understand me," or "they're the only people who get me." Attacking friends reinforces the strength of that friendship. As teenagers, friends are an extension of themselves, so by trying to point out bad qualities consistently, chances are your daughter will take it personally.

It's not always easy deciphering whether their friends are a bad influence, or they're just "being teenagers." By that, I mean that exploration and acting out, although sometimes bad, is also a part of being a teenager. If you feel unsure, question yourself if your daughter's character and moods are more on the drastic side. Perhaps she's losing or gaining weight too quickly or there are physical changes and she's looking gaunter and more skeletal than normal. Also, did she have hobbies or interests and suddenly has no interest in any of them?

Was she previously good at schoolwork and now you find yourself frequenting the principal's office too often? If these factors are true for your daughter, you need to make time for her.

Keep your conversation positive and think about times in the not too distant past where she had done something that made you proud. Draw her attention to the things you love about her. She will be more willing to open up when you approach the topic with warmth. Focus your conversation on particular behavior traits and not how you feel personally. Don't talk about a specific friend or what she did and keep everything well rounded. For example, rather than stating that her friend Emily seems to be disrespectful to other people, you could mention that you've noticed when she hangs out with Emily, she's more prone to say disrespectful things. This keeps you focusing on a personality trait.

It's also important if she starts acting out in the home that there are clear instructions within your home regarding the consequences of bad behavior—and this shouldn't change because she's a teenager. Reinforce those boundaries and make sure she is aware of what is expected of her in the home. And don't ever forget to reinforce the opposite and that good behavior needs to be noted and rewarded. Encourage her to be involved in things that used to interest her.

Feeling Socially Isolated

This can be very worrisome and teenagers who
struggle to fit into a group of people and find like-
minded individuals feel like an outcast. The longer they
isolate themselves, the lower their self-worth. Getting
time to themselves is not the same as removing themselves from society. It's something you need to address
from the onset to limit the possibility that it will lead to
more detrimental emotions and disorders such as social
anxiety and depression. Try talking to your daughter
and together figure out if there are reasons that may
have led her to this point. Perhaps she's being bullied or
struggling to understand behavioral changes in herself
and others. Talking to her teachers is a great way to
gain some behind-the-scenes information. Remember
that social isolation is not synonymous with feeling
lonely. Feelings of loneliness can be felt when you're
surrounded by other people. Social isolation resonates
with a severe lack of social connections, which in time,
can lead to loneliness.

She may not want to be involved in activities but talk to
her about ones she would be okay with joining and
encourage her to get out with people that share the
same interests as her. Plan times on the weekend when
the family does things together to get her out of the
house and in the fresh air. Don't force any of this

though. Encouragement is necessary but forced outings will make the situation worse.

Bullying

The psychosis behind bullying isn't simple. Some teenagers who seek power and dominance may turn to bullying to obtain it. Many parents may have had a "mean girl" in their school and like the four girls I was afraid of, one specifically shone out above the rest. We can never assume what is going on for these girls. And their bullying tactics through gossip, social pressure, and put-downs could be their own insecurities and the fact they weren't taught at a younger age how to deal with impulse control or managing their anger.

Given teenagers have a desire to climb the social ladder, they may also bully others physically, verbally, sexually or through cyberbullying. This is a means of squashing the competition and diminishing someone else in an effort to put themselves on top. They could also bully a fellow teenager because they're different in some way, or they find life boring and bullying gives them some excitement and drama in their lives, or they suffer abuse in their own home or from other peers.

Identifying if your daughter is a victim isn't easy to spot. You might notice signs of social alienation, or that she lacks enthusiasm to go to school and gets anxious before and after school. Chances are she'll struggle to sleep—even more than is usual for teens. Having that routine time in your lives to openly discuss issues will allow you to talk about them. Verify that your daughter is not at fault. I don't like labels like "victim" or "anxiety" as my own experience tells me they are easily thrown around and equally used as excuses rather than finding solutions. It's easy for teenagers who are suffering in some way to grasp that label rather than working through it. Praise your daughter if she opens up to you as let's face it, getting teenagers to open up about most things is difficult. Many girls will try avoiding telling their parents as they fear involving parents could potentially make things worse.

Reputation and appearance are so integral in a teenager's life so they're sensitive. Sadly, this sensitivity opens them up to mental and emotional bullying more than any other time in their life. In their teen years, they become more aware of gender and race which offers bullies another tool. Bullying is a serious problem and needs to be dealt with carefully. Likely, you'll want to storm to the school and find the culprits, but this action will make your daughter withdraw as being secretive about the issue has been how she's protected herself thus far. Discuss her feelings thoroughly. From there, work on the problem and tell her you'll take action, but not in a way that affects her. Talk to her teachers and discuss a way forward. Base your actions on your daughter's wellbeing and not your feelings.

Socializing during Social Distancing

As the COVID-19 pandemic rolls on, it's taken a big toll on the mental health of teenagers globally. At a time in their life when social connections are paramount, COVID-19 has derailed them and their need to fit in and conform. While they may need to keep social distance, they can still connect on a social level. Time away from their friends during social distancing is known to affect your teenager's sleep, diet and wellbeing.

Staying connected through group chats, social media and other platforms will allow your daughter to hold on to the group connections she needs. It's important during these trying times to be accommodating with social media usage. Things don't need to get out of hand, but you also don't want her feeling depressed in the isolation either. Encourage your daughter to continue interacting in a way that is possible depending on the current restrictions and social distancing proto-col. It comes down to what children do when they are online. While many boys may spend their time playing games, girls are more prone to move towards social media. In times of social distancing, they may focus too much on this and torment themselves over how many "likes" a post receives. Having close friends though that they can still do regular group chats with will allow your daughter to stay connected and boost her mental health as she still feels they are all there for each other. It's not the social distance teens need to do, it's physical distance.

Encourage your daughter as you still want to hear her laughing with her friends, even if it's through video chat. If she's feeling exhausted and depressed over the current situation, get her to arrange a video chat with a close friend. Suggest she has a "pretend" meal with her friend. They could pretend they were out at a café getting milkshakes if that's something they used to do. Each of them has to make it at home and then video chat while drinking it. Explain to her that sharing feelings is important and if she says she's not in the mood, tell her that perhaps her friend is feeling the same and it will give them a chance to share.

Question:

Which of the following incidents addresses your concern about your daughter's actions in an effort to fit in and was most helpful?

1. That she wants to get body piercings and tattoos.

2. That she's choosing her friends over you constantly.
3. That she's started hanging out with the wrong crowd.
4. That she's withdrawing herself from friends and family and becoming isolated.
5. That she might be the victim of bullying at school.

INTENSE EMOTIONS AND MENTAL HEALTH

Teenagers, being overly emotional due to their strengthening prefrontal cortex, can easily fall into emotional and mental stress. A lot is happening in your daughter's life, even if you think she has it too easy as she sits on the couch and complains when she has to set the table at dinner time. Too often we feel compelled to offer our own perspective or jump in with what we believe as sound advice when our teenagers open up to us. The best chance you can give your daughter so that her emotions don't take a downward turn is to listen. Give her the gift of listening. It allows her to feel heard and often, our daughters don't even want our advice. Think about what she's saying and decipher if she is searching for your advice, or simply needs to vent. Don't feel the need to solve her problems for her. She needs to figure it out, and you need to offer support and guidance only.

By dealing with excessive stress with our teenagers, we limit them from falling into anxiety disorders and drug-related abuse. However, I cannot denote enough that stress in all human life is necessary. The media often tells us that stress is bad which confuses everyday stress with chronic stress and anxiety. Society spends countless money on wellness products and techniques to pursue an unreasonable belief that chasing happiness means not having negative emotions. It's not about eliminating stress; it's about learning to manage it.

Remember that a teenager's childhood mind is only beginning to understand the adult world. When you take into consideration friends, the pressure of school, the unforeseeable future, their annoying parents, politics, climate change, and racial and sexual issues, it can be quite an overload. They can easily feel overwhelmed as they don't know how to take it all in and express how they feel about it in the same process. With nowhere to offload their emotions, it will boil internally, and you end up with an erratic and moody daughter.

Keep an eye on sudden changes in your daughter and this can be a good indication that her current emotions and stress levels are higher than is normal for a teenager. Perhaps she used to be highly active and motivated and all of a sudden she doesn't want to go anywhere except her room. Maybe she can't seem to remember household responsibilities or procrastinate beyond reasoning over her homework, or she suddenly eats too much or too little. When your daughter appears to be the complete opposite, this is cause for alarm. Feelings of stress and anxiety often cause headaches and stomachaches so if she's feeling sick constantly, there's a possibility her stress is causing physical symptoms.

Dealing with everyday stress for adults is part of life. As teenagers, they need to learn and develop their stress management skills. Stress comes about as a person doesn't feel they have the necessary resources to get themselves out of something they deem difficult, dangerous, or painful. This feeling of drowning in their own inability is overwhelming. The mechanism in our body that switches stress on, switches it off. Therefore, stress is necessary, in small manageable ways. I cannot express enough how critical it is that you don't hover over your daughter's every move and solve all her problems. By doing that, she will never strengthen her own ability to deal with stress. Confusing normal and necessary stress responses in teenagers should not be confused with anxiety disorders. This way of thinking will lead parents to believe that normal negative emotions to the world around them equate with mental disorders which is not the case.

Your daughter needs to learn through trial and error, but any period of extreme angst is not required for her development. Both positive and negative emotions are experienced during teenage years and while these are not signs of mental illness, they can lead to it if she doesn't learn the necessary skills. Don't fool yourself into believing teenagers are fragile, as they aren't. They should also become familiar with failure as it happens throughout our lives. There is a fine line between "normal functioning" and disorders and it's critical not to jump the gun. Making your daughter believe, because you think so, that she is suffering from an anxiety disorder offers a negative impact on her ability to develop an age-appropriate resilience.

Frustration with the World

As parents, we understand that parenting doesn't end with adolescence as history dictated. We help our children traverse through life and all its epic challenges. And we understand that the kind of relationship we have with our daughters during their teenage years impacts how they weave their way through. Studies from many teenagers indicate that a large part of how they experienced their teenage years was due to how they were brought up.

But let's be honest, teenagers can be frustrating at the best and worst of times. Too many conversations need to begin and end with an argument to validate their opinion which strangely always needs to be the opposite of yours. While they're beginning to understand how to form arguments to validate an opinion, they don't yet understand the ability to view life from a variety of perspectives—such as absolutely anyone else's other than their own. This is a natural process, yet it leaves them frustrated with themselves, you, and the world around them. Having argumentative skills are precisely that, skills that one must learn.

Have you ever been in a situation where you've geared your daughter up for when everyone needs to be ready and leave the house for a family dinner? You even go so far as to remind everyone beforehand that there's half an hour left so they need to be out the door then. When you want to lock the door as all other family members are in the car and waiting, you notice your daughter is nowhere in sight. You sigh deeply and find her sitting on her bed and staring out the window, undressed, and far from ready to go. It can be beyond infuriating. An array of clothes is on the floor and her response will be something non-sensible such as "I can't go. I don't have anything to wear." You grind your teeth as this is the last thing you need right now when everyone else in the family is waiting in the car. Her seemingly selfish behavior has no end, and you take a deep breath.

You take in the clothes strewn across the floor and wonder if she doesn't perhaps have too many options and that's where the problem begins and ends. You know if you yell at her she's going to throw something on in anger and for the entire family outing she'll be miserable, make sure everyone knows it, and ruin the day for everyone involved. And that's the last thing you need. It's not that she's unable to make decisions. She's very capable. The problem is that she cannot master the ability to imagine hypothetical situations. The problem is not what she should wear, but what is the ideal and best answer as there cannot be any in-betweens. This cycle of brooding indecision leads to worrying and the more she worries, the more she doubts herself over making the correct decision. In an effort to avoid failure, she simply won't make a decision at all.

From my own experience, it's too easy to lose your cool in these situations, especially when time is ticking away. Don't belittle her when small decisions are massive dilemmas. You'll only exacerbate her surmounting anxiety. Help guide her through. Does she want to wear something comfortable? What color is she in the mood for? Consider where she's going and what would be appropriate. Guide her to ask herself these questions so she can slowly solve the problem on her own. One way of teaching them this skill is encouraging them to give thought to their opinion before voicing it. Teach them to be respectful to whomever they're talking to while at the same time expressing themselves and listening to the other person, who may also have their own opinion.

Intense Emotions

It's relatively common knowledge that teen daughters undergo great emotional swings. It could be day-to-day, or they could experience a whole range of emotional swings within a day.

Teenagers experience intense emotions throughout their teen years. Yes, their brain does become better developed at dealing with emotions, but that only happens if they learn the tools to cope with them. Coping with emotions comes down to strategies they learn to break them down and understand them.

Emotions are thrown at us throughout our lives, regardless of age. What changes are our coping skills. Your daughter is undergoing hormonal changes, new life experiences and her independence is shifting as she begins to take in her view on life in a different manner.

Consider yourself for a moment. I guarantee you have days where you're so exhausted and overwhelmed with everything life seems to be throwing in your direction, but you pull through, still manage to do everything required of you for the family and then fall to sleep, utterly exhausted. Now imagine the same thing for your daughter who has little life experience to understand that despite what life throws at you, you still need to do what is required.

Helping her through these intense emotions is about understanding what she likes doing and encouraging her to take on challenging activities that will allow her to set and reach goals. Music, as an example, is a great way of releasing emotions. Perhaps she's always wanted to learn an instrument. Now might be a great time to start!

Talking to her and making sure she understands that these tumultuous emotions are normal will help her. She's likely just as frustrated with herself and telling her it's all part of growing up and hormonal changes will allow her to realize there's nothing wrong with what she's experiencing. The best way to do this is to be open about your own feelings and emotions when you aren't feeling that great either.

When you see your daughter is down in the dumps about something, have a plan of action to tackle it. Perhaps there is a favorite song you know she likes listening to. Play it and turn the volume up so she can hear it wafting into her room. Perhaps you can both walk the dog together and get some fresh air. And if all fails, go up to her and give her a hug. Words aren't always necessary; this will allow her to understand you care.

Unmotivated Behavior

Think of times in your life where there was so much going on and you felt as though control was out of your grasp as everything swam around out of your reach. You longed for it to stop. You longed to crawl into bed and pull the covers over your head in a vague attempt at pretending the world didn't exist. Resistance is a funny thing. This hiding away from reality can seem as though your daughter is unmotivated about life. Yet when it comes to her friends, she has all the motivation in the world—so it seems impossible to accept her behavior. The more wisdom you try to sell, the less she's interested in buying. It isn't that she definitely wants to go against what you're selling, she's simply motivated to do one thing, and that is resisting. It might be about schoolwork, assignments, or activities. This resistance is a power play, and it isn't that she's not interested in what you're selling, but rather she feels powerless. She rarely understands what's going on inside her head, so she attempts to withhold, in much the same manner as you when everything is spiraling out of control and you long to shut the world out. When you try to coax her back into the world in a positive way, she sees your attempts as controlling.

We're all motivated by something. The question is . . . what? You want to change the outlook that teenagers are motivated to do nothing which goes against what you want. This attitude is born from still learning appropriate social and problem-solving skills. They don't always feel comfortable in their changing body, or how to deal with other people's behavior and meeting what they consider your demands and expectations of them.

Don't tell yourself they're hopeless victims of their time and resign your thoughts to a failed society of 21st-century children. This doesn't help. They aren't victims, they're just trying to understand life. Think about what your daughter is achieving currently, and therefore something she motivates herself to do. Our job is to help them find other ways to solve the problem of what feels powerless. When challenging motivation, don't yell or argue as that will never solve the problem, only perpetuate it into a never-ending cycle. When you yell, you provide power to their resistance. Remain, to the best of your abilities, calm and precise. Reiterate what you want your daughter to do and then leave her and give her the opportunity to do so. If she is still resisting, make sure she is aware of the consequences of her behavior. If she doesn't care, that's fine. She will care once she has to deal with those consequences.

So, what are good consequences to set? You want to have consequences that not only teach them problem-solving skills but also encourage them to be motivated. Natural consequences work well for teenagers, and as parents, they are not easy to give as you don't want your children to fail. Yet even as adults, we face natural consequences daily. If you're in a hurry and speeding and get pulled over by the police, you can't be angry. You were speeding and that is the natural consequence due to a choice made by you. You failed to take responsibility. Your daughter is doing the same. If she's struggling to study for a test or do her homework, give her the option. Tell her it's her choice if she completes her homework or not. Tell her that there will be no screen time until she does. Tell her if she wants to get in trouble with the teacher, it is also her choice. From there, let her figure out what the best option is going to be. If she does her homework, don't forget to congratulate her on making the right choice. If she doesn't and gets in trouble for it, she'll know that it was her own doing that put her in that situation.

Avoid Helicopter Parenting

Helicopter parenting is a style of parenting that typifies parents who assume if they remove situations that could negatively affect their teenager's life, they won't suffer. Understanding that teenagers cannot learn when we put a safety cocoon around them puts us, and them, on the right path. Never forget that stress, anxiety, problem-solving and learning life skills are a way of encouraging them to embrace life—not its uncertainties. Without set guidelines and boundaries from a parent, the relationship can become diffused, and your daughter will struggle in her autonomous development. We've all had helicopter moments as parents, but if you continuously step in and do things for your daughter that she could have and should have done for herself, it is detrimental to her wellbeing.

Helicopter parenting is all about tackling your daughter's battles for her. Many parents who take on this parenting style will say they do it out of love as they don't want to see their daughter hurt and that is true— it is done out of love. Yet you want her to be a strong individual who can traverse this world on her own one day. Hovering over her every move will not empower her to learn the skills to make that happen.

Are you a parent who checks your daughter's grades more than is necessary, pushing more than you should about the classes you think she should take, or ask about every minute of her day after school so you can update yourself on her mental and social wellbeing? Or perhaps she didn't do her homework. And even though she knew it had to be done, you quickly pick up pen and paper and write a note to excuse her. You do every bit of it because your love for her is unwavering. The reality is while she loves you doing it for her as it gets her out of trouble, it doesn't teach her anything positive about her actions. Allow her to learn from the situation and realize that even though she may not have done it because she didn't feel confident in that subject, the world doesn't end when she messes up. Addressing consequences and challenges is part of becoming a resilient adult.

When you have input in all her decision-making, it doesn't allow her to successfully master problem-solving skills. You're inhibiting the strengthening of the prefrontal lobes by taking charge more than required. Our brain is like any other body muscle, and it is strengthened through utilization. The more we attempt problem-solving, the better and stronger we become.

If you forever hover over your child throughout their emotions and do not teach them to work through them and benefitting from lessons learned from failure, they may lack the ability to self-regulate. They may also tend to act out more than is necessary as they haven't mastered what is perceived as normal emotional outbursts. It encourages, in those teen years, emotional imbalance. What you subconsciously tell your daughter is that you don't think she's capable of handling things and making decisions, so you'll do it for her.

Moving away from *helicoptering* doesn't mean you're letting her sink or swim. It's about balance and guidance. It can be hard to figure out where to start as no parent wants to see their child floundering in the unknown. The first way to stop yourself is the next time your daughter comes to you with a problem or task, don't solve it for her. Instead, listen. Then, ask her how the problem makes her feel and if she can think of any way around it. Start opening the door for her to own her emotions and outcomes. Get into the habit of constantly asking yourself before you interfere, "What's the worst thing that could happen?" If you feel she could be hurt, then ask yourself, "Would she recover from it?" And if she will, even though she would be hurt in the process, allow her to experience the disappointment. Naturally, if we're talking about physical harm, then interfere.

As people, we need to value our own self-worth and a fundamental way to strengthen that is learning resiliency and being able to bounce back from down-falls and setbacks. Many teenagers today lack the "know-how" when it comes to leaving home and making it by themselves at college or in the workforce purely due to an abundance of parental intervention. Support your daughter, but don't rescue her over the small, and very important failures that life throws in her direction.

Anxiety Disorders

By mid-teens, females are twice as likely to be diag-nosed with an anxiety disorder than males. When do everyday stress and anxiety become a disorder that needs to be addressed? When it becomes overwhelming and unmanageable. An anxiety disorder is a mental illness that disturbs a patient's emotional life, and it will slowly impact every aspect of their life the more it's ignored. If your daughter's anxiety is starting to impact her normal activities in an attempt to avoid feeling anxiety, this isn't positive. She may understand that she's feeling anxious, but the levels are at a point where she feels trapped by her thoughts and feelings.

Sadly, children that reach the point of a disorder have often been struggling with anxiety for some time before parents see the signs. Overprocessing internal aspects is problematic, and not only does it take a lot for symptoms to show, but it also takes a long time for your daughter to understand that her thinking and emotions aren't on par with others. Telling your daughter "Don't worry, you'll be fine" achieves absolutely zilch. If she's been dealing with an anxiety disorder for some time, chances are, over the years she's built up a whole lifestyle to work her way around it subconsciously. There are likely activities she does and doesn't choose, or friends she feels comfortable with; the limitations she sets for herself that she has instilled in family members and teachers to go along with. She's slowly worked around it for years and everyone around her has gone along with it as no one knew she had any emotional misunderstandings. This is why treating an anxiety disorder is difficult as the longer a child has been dealing with it, the deeper her coping mechanisms are ingrained in her personality. What is necessary from here on is not eradicating anxiety but teaching your daughter how to deal with it more efficiently.

Threat vs. Challenge

The first step is teaching the brain to understand that the situations that cause those feelings of anxiety (triggers) need to be recognized. Perhaps your daughter suffers social anxiety, so when the room fills with more people than she can handle, the trigger is released, and her body feeds off anxiety. For her, it's a severe threat, as if she were facing a hungry lion. Rewiring her brain to understand that it's not a threat but a challenge is the first step in working through her disorder. With the mindset that something is a challenge, she will naturally approach it in a way where she's eager to solve the problem. She'll tell herself, "You've got this." On the opposite side of the scale, a lion is standing in front of her. Her mind is screaming, "Run! run!"

For your daughter to understand the difference, it's not simple. Her thought patterns could have been years in the making, and it will be an ongoing effort to rewire her brain. Talk to her teachers about her situation or coaches if she has sports activities. At home is when you can focus on her anxiety the most. Work with her in questioning herself. When she can feel herself becoming stressed and worked up about something, she needs to consciously be aware of it and force herself to appraise the situation.

- Will this situation cause me harm, or can I benefit?
- Can I handle this situation?

She needs to rewire her brain and tell it, "You can do this!" The more that rewiring is worked on, the stronger the connection will become. It's about changing her appraisal of a situation and turning the physiological response from stress to excitement as that process will naturally force the body to prepare itself for success. What she needs to master is that she needs the adrenaline and hormone boost to focus, but she doesn't need the mindless head chatter telling her she'll fail and deterring her from success.

Tell her to consider her strengths in situations, not her weaknesses. It's about rising to a challenge. Be sure she understands those butterflies in her stomach are perfectly normal and the reason they're there is to help her deal with situations better. Changing her auto-mated response that there is an obstacle in front of her to using it as a catalyst are mindsets she needs to control. Feeling nervous is okay. It shows she cares and that is important.

Controlled Breathing

Anxiety can often cause a person to feel breathless, whether you have a disorder or not. If your daughter is suffering from a disorder, this can lead to a perpetual feeling of breathlessness. If she's breathless from basic chores, this is a sign there may be a problem. If your daughter doesn't know 100% what causes her anxiety— especially if she's suffering from general anxiety disorder—paying attention to when her breathing becomes irregular is a great place to start. When she is feeling out of breath, what was her thought process in the past hour prior to that? Perhaps in her analysis, she can identify a trigger.

Changing the way your daughter breathes will help her manage anxiety. She may not believe it, but the benefits of proper breathing have been widely documented. A person can literally bring on anxiety symptoms by overbreathing. When we breathe quickly, the amount of carbon dioxide decreases in our lungs. This can cause the physical symptoms associated with anxiety. For your daughter, it will feel like a natural step to breathe more given she's feeling breathless. Ironically, this process exacerbates the physical and mental feelings of anxiety and makes it worse. Slowing down her breathing is what will help, even though in the moment it will feel counterintuitive. When the imbalance of oxygen to carbon dioxide in the blood passes a threshold, it causes feelings of anxiety, tingling fingers, headaches, chest pains, or dizziness.

Practice some breathing and relaxation techniques with your daughter. Find a quiet place and sit upright with your neck, shoulders and back well supported.

- Place a flat hand on your belly and let out a cough. The muscle that moves is the diaphragm.
- Breathe in slowly through your nose, feeling the diaphragm move under your hand as you draw in air down into your belly.
- Breathe out through your nose slowly, making the breathing out motion twice as long as the breathing in motion.

Get your daughter to master this technique and do it several times a day for at least five minutes each time.

In moments where she feels high levels of anxiety set in, she needs to be able to withdraw herself to a quiet spot—so her teachers need to be aware. This could be in the toilet at school; what matters is that she's alone and doesn't feel anyone is watching her. To relax herself, she needs to try this breathing technique. It may take some time to get used to this technique, so practicing at home as well is a great option.

- Sit comfortably, supporting shoulders, neck and back and close the eyes.
- Start by breathing air out of the body first.
- Then, breathe in through your nose as much as needed.

- When breathing out slowly again through your nose, let out a controlled sigh in the process. It may sound long and an eternal groan. When breathing out that sigh, imagine the noise created by the sigh is all the tension leaving the body. Focus on it draining away and continue to breathe evenly.
- Do this several times until feeling more relaxed.
- From there, continue breathing in and out slowly and begin thinking about the body from the toes upward and relaxing the muscles.
- Think about toes, ankles, knees, thighs, and hips. Imagine all the muscles relaxing.
- Think about abdominal and back muscles and relax them.
- Keep working upwards through the fingers, arms, and shoulders.
- From the shoulders, move up to the neck, allowing the head to rest forwards or backwards—depending on comfort.
- Now think about the face muscles and allow every part to relax.
- Remain in this calm and relaxed position, breathing in and out slowly. Let the tension go.
- If the mind is instantly active in this position, focus on which parts of the body have tensed

themselves and start the process of relaxing them again.

- Once remaining in this relaxed state for several minutes without the mind racing off somewhere, then slowly get up.

The Three Fundamentals

Your daughter may have heard you go on about sleep, nutrition, and exercise before, and the conversation makes her irritable. All these fundamental require-ments can be affected by anxiety disorders. They can even instigate a disorder when the needs are not met. When your daughter reaches her teenage years, the release of melatonin to get her to sleep begins releasing later in the evening which is why they don't seem tired when they should be going to bed. Early school morn-ings mean they rarely, if not ever, get their required eight to ten hours of sleep each night. Sleep deprivation can impact mental wellbeing and increase the risk of anxiety and lower self-esteem. Once those areas are affected, a natural occurrence is that your daughter's academic performance will also be affected.

She's in a difficult situation as I'm sure she understands she feels better with sleep, but she quite simply isn't tired. Talk to her. Brainstorm together what might work best so she gets a good night's rest. Make a decision together what time bed should be and how long before bed all screens should be put to rest, and she should read a book or do something tranquil to encourage sleep. Some children get surplus homework and projects from school, so working together on time schedules also allows her to have enough time to unwind each day as well. No teenager enjoys taking an afternoon nap but encouraging her to take ten minutes after school to lay on her bed, with no screen, and just relaxing can do wonders. Other tips include having a warm chamomile tea before bedtime. Make sure the bedroom is dark each night and there are no on/off lights leaking into the room such as lights from charging devices. Work on getting her brain into wiring itself into a routine that works for her.

- Do the same thing, each night, before going to bed. For example, read 15 minutes, have a tea, do some relaxing breathing, then sleep.
- Set this on repeat for four weeks.
- After a month, continue the same routine, but move it back 15 minutes so that she essentially goes to bed earlier.
- Do this for one week.
- After a week, do exactly the same thing, but moving backward another 15 minutes.

- Do this until the going to sleep process gives enough sleep for the time she wakes up.
- It's also important to be active during the day so that it helps to physically wear her out.

The idea when it comes to healthy eating is not because you want to dictate what she will and won't eat. It's about teaching her the fundamentals of a healthy body so that she makes the choice on her own to eat healthily. Most teens and adults know what we should be eating, but it doesn't mean we do. The best way to begin is simply to not make things accessible. It's much easier to grab a heap of packaged foods and snacks from the cupboard than making a healthy sandwich. Not having all those unhealthy snacks available is the simplest approach.

For snacks after school or even breakfast, rearrange your fridge. Make the foods you want her to eat to be the most visible and readily available such as boiled eggs, cheese wedges or yogurts. When I was encouraging my girls to make healthier choices, I started by taking things out of the fridge that I wanted them to have for lunch. It was always a selection of fruits, cheeses, meats, etc. They had to choose from those options only. Eventually, when I stopped placing it all on the bench, they would move towards the same type of foods as they had come to enjoy eating them.

Another way to encourage positive food habits is in the food preparation and planning itself. Get your daughter to be part of the food shopping and unpacking. If you plan your meals during the week, then do it together so she can see that you always consider food in a balanced way when meal planning. My daughters had to take turns between Monday and Thursday evenings. On Monday and Wednesday, one daughter had to help me cook the dinner. On Tuesday and Thursday, the other daughter had to help me. Over the weekends, I had more time on my hands and my husband and I enjoyed cooking together on those days.

With an anxiety disorder, the aspect of physical activity might seem like an insurmountable feat. One of my daughter's suffered low muscle tone from birth so this made my life even harder to get her motivated and moving. As much as I would talk, her motivational efforts would last perhaps a week and dwindle into nothing afterwards. Like many things for us parents, being a good role model is often the best approach. Don't single her out and instead make the activity a family effort. Show her that healthier choices are necessary for everyone in the family, not just her. The best way of building healthy habits is by starting with small actions that are easily repeatable. If you take her to the gym and she utterly exhausts herself, she's not going to be happy to go back. Lower your expectations. Start small.

Before you begin cooking dinner, ask her to take the dog, for example, on a 10-minute walk down the street. This is not grueling, but it's still an activity that makes her get outdoors. Establish the routine first before adding onto it. Stick with a limited time for several weeks, then add another 10 minutes onto it. Over time, she'll build confidence and appreciate the relaxed state of being that fresh air naturally provides us with.

Be Mindful

When an anxiety attack is in full swing, often what happens is your daughter is reacting to past or future outcomes. The trigger will make her act instinctively without considering where her emotions are coming from. If she can learn to be aware, or mindful of her immediate surroundings, she can then teach herself to react and perceive the threat differently. Allowing herself to think in the "now" will counter her ruminating and worrying about what happened half an hour ago or what she believes will happen an hour from then. I should have done this or that is a maladaptive thinking process. Yes, experiences teach us things, but being stagnant in that process doesn't teach us anything. When she is actively conscious of her feelings and emotions, she is better able to identify and process them.

Whether your daughter suffers social anxiety or is obsessed about academic results or self-ruminates herself to the point of general anxiety disorder, all of these can be helped with a mindful approach. Being mindful, when she can master it, will naturally make her more centered, happier and less depressed. It has a direct positive association with countering anxiety. Some people may take on yoga or tai chi to learn mindfulness meditation. If that doesn't interest your daughter, go back to breathing techniques. Concentrate on breathing in and out slowly through the nose with lips closed, even if a crowd of people is standing in front of her. When her mind reverts to her worries, she needs to focus on her breathing again. Right now, in that very moment as she breathes, she needs to tell herself it feels wonderful to be alive.

Clinical Depression

Anxiety can lead to depression and like anxiety, there are different levels of depression. Clinical depression (also known as major depressive disorder) is a severe form of depression where the mood is low consistently —as if the rain cloud above your daughter's head never leaves regardless of the time of day, or internal and external influences. When considering your daughter, think about how drastic the pendulum of her mood swings is. Is she experiencing major academic problems and a severe lack of concentration which is unusual for her? Was she confident before and now she feels the need to hide herself away as if she feels ugly and unworthy? Some teenagers are known to have clinical depression as a result of being addicted to their phones and social media—given it often increases isolation and depression.

A friend of mine's son suffered from depression. She had very strict rules about screen time when it came to his PlayStation and what days he could play and for what lengths of time. When lockdowns began due to COVID-19 and the schools closed, he was cut off from the friends who made him feel life was worth living. It was the one time his psychologist told his mom not to be so regimented with screen time. It may not be ideal, but if that is the only outlet a person has to connect and connections are a lifeline for them, taking it away isn't ideal.

You know your daughter and you know what is perceived as "normal." If things seem drastically out of character, and not what you can pass off as hormonal outbursts in a teenager, it's critical that you address the situation. If she's bursting into tears over the smallest things, constantly plagued by aches and pains, and is extremely sensitive to criticism as if she is an under-achiever, it opens the pathway of communication. Depression is a serious disorder and can lead to suicidal thoughts. Don't tell yourself "she'll get over it" as this is critical—meaning symptoms don't disappear. Don't start your conversation off by labeling her because that's what you diagnosed the situation to mean. Talk about what you may have read as clinical depression symptoms and that you've noticed some things she does that concern you. Ask her if she agrees and if there are things she's going through. Tell her perhaps you weren't there as much as you should have to listen to her and for that you're sorry, but you are ready to listen. Don't have a list of questions as if you're probing, simply make sure she understands you're there for her.

Even if your daughter's personality leans to introversion, isolation during depression can be devastating. Make it a priority each day to set time aside to talk with her. Being in a social setting is a natural mood uplifter. If you cannot get her to engage in such activities, make sure she connects with your face regularly. It may seem like a daunting topic but discussing depression and suicide with your daughter doesn't make things worse. Instead, it shows that you're open to her emotions and are willing to tackle those hard subjects with her. However, while approaching the subjects is great, don't push them.

In the same way as with anxiety disorders, sleep, nutrition, and exercise are essential tools in mitigating stress and anxiety. It doesn't take much to walk ten minutes a day and even if your daughter does it slowly, it will still be beneficial. If you don't understand much about depression yourself and you think much of it is just in her head, you need to change your mindset. You love your daughter. Do you truly think she would bring this all on herself when she's entering the most exciting time of her life? Be there for her. Support, listen and understand. It's not easy as the parent, but it's even harder for her.

If you fear your daughter may be clinically depressed, trust your gut instinct. If you feel you've done all you can but are afraid there are still unsolved issues, don't be afraid to turn to others for help whether it be teachers at her school or mental health professionals. If you do take her to a health professional, make sure she feels she connects with the person. If teenagers don't really like the professional, they aren't going to open up enough to get to the bottom of problems. If you need to try out a few specialists until your daughter finds one she can relate to, that's okay.

Don't disregard and throw all the household routines out the window. Instead, the routine of normality will give your daughter something to hold on to that she knows is constant and required. However, relax a little in other areas. Perhaps your normal parenting style has consequences for forgetting homework or really bad test marks. Depression isn't a free pass for bad behavior but understanding the effects depression can cause vs. wrongdoing is two different things.

Eating Disorders

Many teenage girls are affected by eating disorders. Most that are, are often already 15% under their ideal body weight. They have a low self-image and blame their weight on that image. Like many disorders, there is no one thing you can blame for the disorder beginning. Our teenagers are all different and for one, it could be family relationships and for another, they may have other psychological problems. For some, they strive for perfection, such as in gymnastics or ballet, and these types of sports are often linked with anorexia. If an eating disorder is left unaddressed, it can significantly impair physical, social, and emotional health and even lead to death.

Preventing such disorders begins with open communication. Make sure early on that your daughter is aware of healthy eating habits and body image. Teach these things to her before she enters her tweens. The earlier the better. Talking to her about good eating habits and exercise affects internal and external health. Eating dinner together as a family is important for many reasons and stopping eating disorders is one of them. If you and your daughter see television shows or advertisements that highlight body types, use that as a way of communicating and talking to her about different body types and how seeing things like that makes her feel.

The healthier your daughter's body image is of herself and the higher her self-esteem, the less chance she has of developing an eating disorder. If she approaches you in her early teens about dieting, make sure she realizes that dieting isn't healthy and especially in her early years, can compromise her growth and health. Make sure she understands that food should not be linked with emotions, and it's important for you as mother to lead by example.

If your daughter is seeking medical help for her eating disorder, talk to the health professional for advice on eating and coping with mealtimes. Make plans together over what she's happy to eat in an effort to get her back on the right eating plan. If there are other siblings, and your partner, make sure that everyone is aware of what is going on and that no one is allowed to make silly jokes about weight, food serving sizes, calories and basically anything food-related. She would take any mention as a personal affront.

Try to make the family mealtime fun. Don't force conversations but try to have light and entertaining topics that are not detrimental in any way. After dinner, encourage watching a movie together as this is a great distraction from her either wanting to throw up or go exercising to get rid of every calorie she devoured.

Substance Abuse

Drinking alcohol, binge drinking, taking drugs or prescription drugs hinders teenager's decision-making skills. Their underdeveloped reasoning areas of the brain are not yet in control in mastering impulse control. Alcohol and drugs impair this ability even more so, which could lead them to sexual acts before or after substance use.

Your daughter may turn to substance abuse for various reasons such as peer pressure, external stressors allowing her to feel that drinking or smoking may allow her to let off steam, or a misguided way of lashing out at parents when striving for independence. Why do they do it? Well, in many ways, it's natural. In teenagers, dopamine is released at high levels and this hormone pushes the brain to seek new rewards. Often, these are found through risky behavior. It is also more likely drinking or smoking will be done in peer groups, and not alone.

Taking into consideration the prefrontal cortex, when you add alcohol and substance abuse to the concoction, your daughter is likely to make worse decisions than ever before which could lead to sexual endeavors or getting into a car with drunk peers. The aspect of analyzing is thrown out the window and in that moment, it's all about the thrill.

Encouraging your daughter early in her teens and talking openly about substance abuse is necessary. Without helicopter parenting, know where your daughter is and who her friends are. Talk about reckless behavior and set out rules and consequences, like all other aspects. Tell her they are in place because you care, not because you're judging her inabilities. Make sure you both agree on those rules and talk about options. Teach her about the harm of mixing alcohol and drugs or even mixing different drinks. In the same process, make sure she's knowledgeable about "better" ways to drink and partying safely if a party comes along and the peer pressure of the moment takes control.

- Why this time? Why does she want to drink, and will it help or make things worse?
- Has she eaten to reduce alcohol absorption?
- What does she plan on drinking and what is the alcohol percentage? Know her personal limit.

- Never take a drink from other people and never leave her drinking unattended.
- Never move away from the company of friends.
- Make sure she can always contact you as a safe way to come home.
- Take a condom if she is thinking sexual activity is on the cards. You don't want that, but in the worst-case scenario, you want her to be protected.
- Safe consumption would be to slowly sip on a glass of water before getting another drink.

Building Self-Esteem & Confidence

Your daughter's confidence during her teenage years has a direct correlation with her mental health. The lower her self-esteem, the less likely she'll feel able to adapt and fit in and the more likely she'll be willing to throw away her morals. She will have a harder time standing up for herself and is more likely to give in easily. The more confident she is, the stronger she will be when it comes to what she knows is right and wrong.

Taking steps throughout her teenage years is necessary so she can successfully guide herself through peer pressure, relationships and friendships, and making well-thought-through decisions. One of my daughters would drive me crazy through her ability in putting herself down. In her youth, she'd always been apt at math. In her teens, she still was. Yet when they were learning something new, rather than working through it, her mood would sour, and she'd give up and tell herself she wasn't intelligent enough. Nothing other than perfection, even in math was enough for her. Teaching her to balance self-acceptance and self-improvement was necessary for the boost in confidence. I had to teach my daughter that flaws are normal and to rather take them on board, and work at improving instead of labeling herself as silly.

A great idea when it comes to confidence is to talk with your daughter. What does she believe are her strengths and weaknesses? Get her to write them down. When she looks at her weaknesses, ask her to pick three she feels are the most important ones to improve on. Together, come up with some goal-setting strategies that will strengthen her problem-solving skills in the process that makes her address these areas she would like to improve on. Don't set unachievable goals, that will only lead, in her mind, to more failure. Understanding that she can always control the amount of effort put in, but not the outcome is a necessary rule to learn so she doesn't feel confidence is lost every time she thought she did not nail a test.

Another fun way to do this together is by utilizing the four-color personality test. Some basics on how this works can be found on: https://truecolorsintl.com/the-four-color-personalities/. All the colors have positives and negatives of a personality type, and you can see if your daughter agrees with the negatives on the chart. You can try to work out some plans based on those.

Teaching and encouraging your daughter to be respect-fully assertive offers a better opportunity to when she struggles personally, physically or academically, she'll speak up about it. If she can learn that her feelings and thoughts are validated and she has a right to open up about them, it offers her a larger chance of not being swayed by peers when she doesn't agree with some-thing. The best way to encourage this is by allowing her to have choices. When she understands the value of having a choice, she'll learn that she doesn't have to say yes to something because she was told to.

She will always use you as the role model. So, talking badly about your own body and confidence, means she'll possibly take on those traits too. If you're forever worrying about your weight and going on diets, she'll grow up believing that as a female that's what you do. Building confidence is about talking about times of triumph and when you've done things that made you proud. Make sure to teach her about loving her body and that it is natural as she goes through puberty for her body shape and size to change. Holding on to the idea that she'll always fit into a certain jeans size will increase self-loathing.

I understand that social media is here to stay, but it's a tightrope balance when it comes to how much it can detriment your daughter's self-esteem. When self-esteem is already low, teenagers put all their validation into comments and likes on posts. They build them-selves up on external circumstances they have no control over. Teaching your daughter worth is about being out there in the world, learning and finding values she believes in. It's sometimes impossible to tell your daughter that a caring nature is more important than looks, body image, or superficial aspects—espe-cially when she wants to look appealing and fit in. Getting her involved in some social activities will help with this such as helping alongside you at a food bank or animal shelter one night a week. Learning empathy and compassion goes a long way in our internal image of ourselves.

Many advertising and marketing platforms sell girls a distorted view of what a woman is and should be. Talk with her and get her to be critical and question what she sees. Teach her about the ideal of perfection in media terms and how much work through posing, lighting, makeup, photoshop editing and airbrushing it takes for that photograph to appear as drop-dead gorgeous as it does. Opposed to that mindset is that while there are a plethora of industries that demand her attention in looking good, there are as many that make incredible profits over her feeling unattractive too. Critical thinking allows her self-worth and confidence to know and understand who she is, not what the outside world demands her to be.

Lastly, talk to her about her inner voice and discuss the power of the brain and that we become what we believe ourselves to be. If she's telling herself how ugly or silly she is, she'll fall into the habit of never believing she could be otherwise. Always give your own positive affirmations when she's done well. It's never about the result, but the effort. When her inner dialogue puts down her intelligence, tell her to recognize it and rephrase that voice and say, "If I work hard, I can do this." The power of positive self-talk will get her through many things in life.

Question:

What's your biggest fear when it comes to your daughter's emotional and mental health and what do you need to focus on the most?

1. That she's struggling to deal with everyday stressors.
2. That she seems to be falling behind at school and feeling unmotivated.
3. That she's anxious constantly and may be suffering from an anxiety disorder.
4. That you're scared she may be depressed
5. That you're concerned she may have an eating disorder or be abusing substances.

DEFIANT TEENAGERS

Remember when your daughter would put on a sweater as you insisted it was cold outside? She may not have wanted to, but she did because you asked her. She needed no other validation except your words. Well, that era of compliance has just left the building. Entering is your loving daughter who attempts to defy all your rules because none of them make sense. Some amount of defiance in a teenager is normal, that's the reality of it; much like stress and anxiety are normal. They're young adults developing mentally and physically. They're also compulsive and led too often by emotions. What they want is to have the same privileges as you, the adult. What they don't understand is they are yet to earn those privileges through experience.

Possibly you've picked your daughter up from school and know she had a trial for the school drama club. You know it meant a lot to her. You ask how it went and she looks at you defiantly and yells, "I don't want to talk about it!" She cuts you down with a low and lethal blow and stares out the car window. Your anger in that moment is seething. You could let your anger take control over how disrespectful she is any way you want to. You've learned a few things along this parenting journey, though, and understand that lectures don't get you far. Instead, say something like "Possibly that was not the best way to express your need for quiet. I suggest you work on it differently next time. Right now, we can be quiet." Chances are she'll begin to feel remorseful over her actions. When your daughter is being defiant against you, sometimes offering nothing in return is best so she can let her belligerence resonate in her own ears.

Testing boundaries and attempting to shatter rules can be challenging. It's important during this time to reassess any previous rules you had in place before your daughter entering her teenage years. Are all those rules still necessary and could you tweak some rules to reflect her growing needs? I'm not saying ditch the rules, as that would be detrimental. When teenagers challenge rules, it's because to them they make no sense at all. The best option is to sit your daughter down and talk. If some rules drive her crazy, ask what those rules are. Talk about why you have them in place and how you believe it is beneficial. Two things can happen. One, you realize that perhaps it doesn't make as much sense as you thought after she offers you her opinion and together you can readjust to agree on something mutually agreeable. Two, she'll understand why you set the rules and while she may still grumble, accept it as she now has a deeper knowledge about the "why."

Even as adults, we can at times be in a situation where we feel our life is out of control. It doesn't matter where we try to focus and gain direction from, everything we reach is too malleable. It can be a very confusing time. This feeling is no different for teenagers. Their life, quite frankly, is out of control biologically. For teenagers who push their defiant boundaries too far, it often comes down to preexisting troubles they haven't faced such as anxiety, depression, family conflict, or past trauma.

When your daughter pushes these boundaries to the point that it disrupts normal family life and functioning, there's likely trouble on the horizon. You don't want her brain to form patterns of current behavior to long-lasting behavior. If she's already showing indications of defying the family, authority, school, and the law, these can easily turn into behavior patterns if not carefully dealt with. It can make you as the parent feel helpless and the strain is massive.

Going Too Far

Have you ever watched the 1983 movie *Risky Business*? It's entertaining. In real life, a teenager's risk-taking escapades are even scarier. The top three causes of death in teens in America are accidents, homicide, and suicide. And in the majority of these cases, they stemmed from risky behavior. Unintentional injuries such as mobile phone usage while driving, a bicycle without a helmet, not wearing a seatbelt, or having access to a firearm are just a few on a long list of possibilities.

We don't want our daughters hurting themselves or others, so why on earth do they put us through it? Think back to your own childhood. Surely you took some risks of your own in those years. Risky behavior often differs between males and females but the reason behind it is the same. They're experimenting to find their place in the world. There are massive amounts of growth and problem-solving skills that can be learned through their risky behavior. Like it or not, going through these trying times is what helps teenagers become well-adjusted and independent adults. Sadly, sometimes these biological yearnings can lead to devastating results.

Accept that you don't have 100% control anymore. You can ground your daughter and dictate what will happen under your roof, but if she wants to sneak out of the house, you can guarantee she will. So, while you have to some extent lost control, which is natural, you can still guide her even from the background. You cannot influence your daughter when you take the stance of doing it from control and punishment. That scenario will cause her to choose her friends over you, always. Don't shame her for risky behavior but try to understand it. The end decision is in her hands, so your relationship and the connection you've built during her life are critical.

Provide your daughter with information rather than sounding as if you're offering a free lecture. And always listen! No matter how much you've prepared yourself and your daughter for this kind of behavior, there's still every chance she may go ahead and do something that surprises her as much as you. What she needs to know is that you're not there to judge and shame her. Shaming is born from criticism and judgment, and when that's all she feels she's hearing from you, she'll distance herself. She'll place the blame anywhere else but, on her shoulders, and say it's your fault because you're a terrible parent, or all her friends are doing it.

Taking risks isn't shameful, so open up about it. Encourage her to take on healthier challenges. Perhaps she's into outdoor activities and you can channel her desires into rock climbing, martial arts, or stage performing. Maybe you've always been strict on hair color, for example, so let her dye her hair blue. The best approach to risky behavior is to simply guide her towards being the wonderful person you want her to be. And the best way to do that is to treat her as if she already is. With the correct guidance, risks can become courageous feats and opportunities Every time she's tested, it forces her to look internally to find personal strength and utilize her growing skills to problem-solve.

Conflict Management

In the end, both parents and teenagers are human, and we suffer human traits—good and bad. No matter how much you empower yourself to be the best parent you can be, there are always going to be times your daughter's antics and behavior derail you. Conflict happens within families just as it does within a group of friends. It's possible that you were in the wrong and said something hurtful as your emotions took center stage. It's equally possible your daughter was at fault and misinterpreted. Either way, you're left with conflict where you're both feeling hurt and angry with each other. One thing you must take on your shoulders in these moments, always, is that you are the parent, and you are responsible for resolving uncomfortable engagements.

If you miss the opportunity to talk about your daughter's mistake or owning up to your own, you potentially widen the gap between you. If she was at fault, make the message clear when you follow up on the argument with her that you love her even though she's done something wrong. If you were at fault, it's imperative you own up to it. Dealing with conflict in this way allows her to see that resolving hurtful issues can come about when we admit fault, take on a position of humility, and ask for forgiveness. She will learn through you that owning up to our mistakes is how we approach situations.

As well as you know your daughter, she knows you too. From the moment she was born she's pushed to ascertain her boundaries and knows when and how hard to push your buttons. There's been symbiosis between you both. However, now that she's questioning your right to authority and beliefs, it's easy to lose your temperament. As parents, we lose our cool often. Showing your daughter that you're not perfect and also vulnerable and sensitive to harsh words teaches her that it's ok to admit to mistakes and failures. There's extreme power in humility.

I've had arguments with my daughters in the past that escalated out of control, and they started with the simplest issue. Before I knew it, there sat a wide chasm between us born from something as frivolous as whether an item was red or pink. In this situation, think about the argument before going back to your daughter and talking. There's a good chance there's a deeper problem she's dealing with like her friends or a boy at school and she's confused and doesn't know what to do. She will naturally take this out on you as you are still her closest ally. She knows you'll forgive her. Ask her to open up if other things are going on in her life she may want to talk about.

While you and your partner may not always agree on the right parenting technique or punishment, tackling conflict needs to be done with a united front. Again, if you're not sure on the best move over an incident, take time out and discuss it together before approaching your daughter on the outcome. For those parents who are divorced or separated, this is tricky as a teenager will divide and conquer effortlessly. Try to align yourself with people in a similar situation such as other single mothers so you have other people to discuss things with. You don't want to be in a situation where doing it alone overwhelms you and detriments your own health either.

Punishment is a tool that is always in your hands to play and no matter what teenagers may be going through, bad behavior isn't excused. If your daughter bad-mouths you, you have every right to tell her, "You aren't allowed to speak to me like that. We can talk about this another time." When you do talk about it, you can take her phone away for one day, so she understands that while you are there for her, you aren't her punching bag. Bad behavior, outside of the home, will always have ramifications. Always return to the scene of the crime and address issues either she or you lost your cool. She's a teenager, so don't downgrade yourself and give her the silent treatment in return. Negotiation and communication are the best tactics.

For her to learn the skills necessary in resolving conflict management, they will help her establish healthy relationships not only with you and her friends but later in life with employers and employees. A lot of the time conflict comes about from not understanding the strong emotions we feel. If you fail to pinpoint what emotions you're feeling, it's hard to understand why you're feeling that way. If you don't understand either of those, then it's almost impossible to communicate effectively to eliminate disagreements.

When your daughter is in control of emotions and understands them, it's easier for her to relay those feelings in a way that doesn't belittle someone else in the process. Conflict needs to be addressed fairly as it's always important to understand it takes two to tango. If your daughter finds herself in conflict often, and not necessarily just with you, try teaching her to take on some of the following tools:

- If she knows she is about to lose her cool, take a two-minute time out rather than saying something she'll regret.
- Treat other people the way she wants to be treated. Try to play her own words back to herself.
- Avoid exaggerating and stick to facts alone as she sees them.
- Be mindful. An argument should never link to a past argument. Always remain in the present.
- Communicate. The silent treatment resolves nothing.

As much as you need to listen to your daughter, you need to teach her that listening is a large part of resolving arguments. There are always two sides, so tell her to look at a problem from another person's perspective. When that person is offering their point of view, she needs to be respectful and listen and not interrupt. Show listening through acknowledgment such as nodding. Active listening isn't easy, even for adults. Yet it certainly helps when it comes to resolving conflict. When both people in the argument stay on high alert, it's often hard to move past this stand-off.

Tell your daughter that sometimes she needs to back down, even if it's only initially. If the other person can see she is offering eye contact, keeping calm and her posture is open to another point of view, these aspects can easily diffuse an exchange. It doesn't mean she accepts defeat when she knows she's right. It simply allows both parties to calm down and from there, a discussion can take place. Make her realize that resolving conflict isn't being a member on the debating team. It isn't about "winning." It's about listening and understanding. I cannot deny I fall into this one myself. I can get so worked up over how on earth something happened and escalated so quickly. I know I'm right. When really, it isn't about being right. It's a matter of altering the mindset that it is not me against my daughter, but rather, both of us against the conflict.

During your daughter's teenage years, there are going to be quite a lot of battles between the two of you. Much like when it comes to a partner, you need to pick your battles. Do you agree with your partner every minute of every day? Most likely not. But that doesn't mean you love them any less. On the same token, you don't have to make a point out of every discretion your daughter commits either. Pick your battles wisely and pay more attention to the bigger things that really matter.

Always remember that the goal of resolving conflict is about finding a resolution. There should be no winners or losers. If your daughter can master that, she has a great chance of success in her life.

Question:

You may have many concerns over your daughter's search for individuality, but what area focuses on your concern the most?

1. That she's taking risks and you're worried about her welfare.
2. That you both seem to be arguing constantly.
3. That she's stopped listening to you and doing as she's told.

5

ATTRACTION & FINDING LOVE

M any things are happening in the lives of a teenager and one that is a clear indication your little girl is growing up is that she searches for love outside the home. When your daughter is a tween or in her early teen years, she'll likely have crushes on boys in her class or go out of her way to watch a particular boy band that plays to her fragile heartstrings. She may talk about a "boyfriend" in her early tween years but don't panic. She's likely at the stage where she may sit with a boy within a social group at school, but not yet ready to be alone with them. Often friend groups are having fun at this stage by pairing and matching everyone together. She may be in her room in the afternoon, staring out the window with longing thoughts of what she understands love to be, but too scared to have a one-on-one date with a boy.

If you find yourself panicking that your 12-year-old wants to go on a date, open up and find out what dating means to her. At this age, it's more of a social status. She and her best friend may both have boys they like and the four may want to go out together. Theoretically, it's not really dating, but four friends going out. It's the ideal way to start interacting with the opposite sex within a group and remove the awkwardness of being alone with a boy. It's like the training wheels you once lovingly attached to your daughter's bike.

Moving into her early teens, your daughter and a boy will likely start moving by chatting to each other constantly via social media, sharing funny images and thoughts. At school, they might have progressed to holding hands and for them, this is a big step in "growing up." Establish early on what your "rules of dating are." What is acceptable to you when it comes to updating you where she is. You know it's a crush, but to her, it's the most epic thing that's happened in her life so don't trivialize the event. You should be having long conversations about dating in these early years. Allowing your daughter to learn about boys and relationships from her friends or social media isn't healthy. Teach her what a healthy relationship is.

Once in high school, these romantic connections can move forward at a scary rate. For a teenager, their first love holds a very special place in their heart and life. The reason many say that a first love is so unforgettable is that given it's the first "adult" connection being made, it will be the only relationship that stays true to innocence and authenticity at the same time. The intense passion in a first love remains in a person's life forever. As the parent, it's a difficult stage to go through but it's about adapting, being respectful to your daughter's feelings, and remaining her confidant should she need you. She may start a topic with you that spirals you into a panic but make a point in that moment to listen, otherwise, you won't offer effective advice. Don't over-protect. Talking about your own feelings with your first love allows her to understand not only that her feelings are normal, but that she can open up and talk to you. Make sure she realizes that a loving relationship teaches us respect for ourselves and others. It's fulfilling, and it's as much about listening and supporting, along with giving and receiving.

If she goes out on a date and you see her in clothes that simply don't cover her body as much as you'd prefer and she has cleavage showing and internally you've let out a scream that heaven could hear, calm down. Look at it this way. She does not have an adult mindset yet. She isn't wearing those clothes to invite the person into bed, but rather, she wants to look grown-up and like a woman. This is completely your call as every parent will have a different standard when it comes to appropriate attire. Generally speaking, discussing her attire in that moment goes against you as the parent. That doesn't mean you shouldn't, as you should talk to her about how she is presenting herself, but in another moment in time. Remember that dressing sexy does not necessarily equal sex.

When it does come to talking about sex with your daughter, make it an open discussion. Don't do this in half measures. It seems ironic really that often girls demand equality in a classroom when it comes to academics and on the field as they want to prove themselves as capable, but behind closed doors or a bedroom, things still differ. Too often behind that door remains a sexist and demeaning cantor that pushes young women to feel as though they should go along with sexual advances—even when they know they don't want to. Talk to her about what she would do if a boy started kissing her. When would she tell him to stop? What if the boy started touching her breasts? What would she do? These are difficult conversations and awkward. Yet, if you make all the effort to teach your daughter life skills, why skip on sex? It will happen eventually, and she needs to know that she should never feel ashamed for saying no, despite how much she's encouraged otherwise. Demystify the pressure you know they will face behind that bedroom door.

Pornography

No matter how much you might put as many blocks as possible on your daughter's devices so pornography doesn't come up, there are always ways around it. There are always friends or other kids at school that view porn and let's face it, most kids are so tech-savvy, if they want to view it, they'll find a way around the blocks you've put in place. Once, Playboy Magazine was as R-rated as you could get. Over the past 20 years, pornography has evolved in leaps and bounds. Once, you had to seek out those fantasies, and today, they are easily accessible, free, varied, and more dangerous than ever.

Many teenage girls might see a naked male for the first time through a friend sending a picture, or she may imagine one through a book she's reading. These are innocent enough and natural thoughts. Often, that initial exposure leads to desire, and is where many sexual fantasies begin. Pornography is a platform where they can see sexual fantasies play out. She knows she shouldn't be watching it and it sets the wrong example for women, but the internal battle in her brain wants the reward of seeing that fantasy.

When girls are exposed to pornography in their early teens, they stop thinking about their grades and activities as they should be. They become exposed to a sexual culture which pushes them to become a consumer of people. Their idea of love and respect becomes distorted. Quite simply, pornography is powerful. And the industry knows it and how it affects teenagers. Let's look at that volatile prefrontal cortex again and consider how motivated it becomes when perceived rewards are offered. Stimulation causes a waterfall effect of memory and motivation. It's like tasting candy for the first time and the brain wants more. That young brain is the ideal sponge for addiction. Like any substance addiction, you need more to reach the initial high. If a teenager looks at pornography for the first time, the brain stores the image. The dopamine that was released sends urgent messages to the brain saying, "More! more!" The more your teenager watches, the more the demand will grow to recreate the same initial feeling.

Sadly, the teenage brain doesn't always understand the difference between reality and media. What does happen, though, is that the child may watch something and experience the desire to act out what they see or desensitize themselves to block it out. This leaves them feeling too little and can lead to detrimental real-life relationships. For many teenage girls what happens with porn is that the fantasy overshadows the actual relationship. Pornographic material affects the mental, emotional, and physical health of a young female, particularly if she already suffers from low self-esteem or mental and emotional issues.

Talking openly with your daughter about pornography is essential. Perhaps you've watched a movie together and there was a slightly provocative scene in it, and this can be the ideal way to open up the conversation. You could start asking her questions about pornography from there. Don't feel as though you're introducing a concept she doesn't know about, as I guarantee she does know it exists even if she's never seen it. Teach her the difference between porn sex and real-life sex. Tell her like in the movie, they are actors being paid. Even if the sex is violent, they're paid to look as though they're enjoying themselves. Many actors have also had body enhancements to make themselves look a certain way. Teenage girls often try to mirror what they see in porn to be attractive to the opposite sex and the industry offers a warped sense of reality—not only of the female body, but the female's complicity in succumbing to a man sexually.

Teach her that in the porn movie, with paid actors, the sex isn't real. She knows that, but she needs to understand that much like the crazy Matrix moves in movies, a real relationship or sexual partner does not work in that way. Real sex comes from emotions, and they are widely void in pornography. Don't leave it too late to have this discussion. If she's ready for a relationship, chances are she knows about porn. And if she's seen it somewhere, her young brain will be thinking that she needs to do what a boy asks her to, even if she feels uncomfortable or degraded. And why? Because what she saw offered the notion that it's the ideal way for a boy to like you. Teaching your daughter the pitfalls of pornography helps her understand sex overall. It may take many conversations, but the more you open up about the topic, the more she'll reciprocate. If she believes you're simply worrying too much or too old to understand love, then search for documentaries or factual scientific videos she can watch. Find a well-made and documented video that discusses the pitfalls of pornography, the chemical effect it has on the brain, and its addiction.

Intimacy, Sex, & Gender Identity

Teenage daughters can be very private, especially when the topic is romance. It can often feel embarrassing for them, and parents, to discuss intimate feelings. They're really just trying to figure out what it all means in their head so while they may pretend they know plenty, your guidance will influence them greatly. Talking about relationships and intimacy needs to happen in the early teenage years with your daughter so that early on she knows her strengths and what she's comfortable with.

Sharing interests with a boyfriend is the way it should be but that doesn't mean she should stop developing her own dreams and personality outside of that relationship. Fine-tuning and identifying her personal likes and dislikes have nothing to do with the partner. Encourage her to keep at least one interest or activity that is "just hers." This will improve her self-esteem and allow her to learn that even while in a romantic relationship, she can still have her own time and needs.

As a parent, you understand the relationship might not last longer than a month. Make sure your daughter knows that the power of friendship doesn't dissolve the moment a boy is on the scene. She may not ever mean for it to happen, but we all know it often does. Teach her that it takes a strong and individual young woman to keep her friends just as close as they are the ones who will always be there for her. If she cannot be herself around a boy or have her own opinion even if it differs from his, suggest that it possibly isn't a good relationship. However, if she's already in a relationship and you're discussing this for the first time, tread carefully. Teens can be defensive if it sounds as if you're criticizing, and you don't want her to turn closer to him in defense over your words. The last thing you need is a Romeo and Juliet situation.

A large part of our daughter's growth is about developing her own sexuality. You can wish that away as much as you want, but it's a natural evolution in life. Teaching her about unwanted pregnancies and sexually transmitted diseases is essential. However, more importantly, is empowering her with what makes good emotional bonds above and beyond the word sex. Allowing your daughter to understand that emotional intimacy comes through knowing and understanding each other offers a whole new dimension to "casual sex." Teach her that sex is special but doing it because she feels pressured will likely leave her feeling empty and alone. Relationships need to be tied in with emotions.

The more your daughter values her self-worth, the more she's prone to making better decisions when it comes to her body. The best way to instill this is through the love and respect you show and give her. She wants to be loved and experience that feeling and if she has a low self-worth, she'll likely do irrational things in the hope of pleasing a boy, hoping he'll be faithful and fall in love with her. When things don't work out, the emotional consequences for her will be devastating and impair her future relationships. Many adults understand that sex doesn't relate to intimacy or an emotional connection, or make a person feel any more or less in love. Many teens haven't learned that yet and may go into sexual encounters only to feel confused and disillusioned afterwards. Your daughter may have given up her body to be left with the same empty feeling she had before sex. The more you talk to your daughter about sex, emotions, and self-worth, is the best way you can develop a healthy young woman who will be better aware of her emotional and sexual feelings.

When you discuss intimacy and sex with your daughter, don't talk about endless negatives such as not falling pregnant or not using protection. Yes, they are discussion points, but telling her about everything she shouldn't be doing isn't really teaching her much. Always include the do's when it comes to sex as like it or not, it will happen. And again, this comes down to empowering her self-worth. You're not being a bad parent if you talk about the positives of sex. Your teenage daughter has those thoughts so remind her that they are natural and not dirty. There is less chance she'll make impulsive choices when she feels safe in the knowledge that it's all part of growing up.

Ideally, by her tween years, you should already be discussing sex, her changing body, and even masturbation. The thought is daunting, I know! And the main reason why is because you want your daughter to remain your innocent angel forever and you don't ever want her to be hurt. And that's ok, we're all in the same boat there. Accept you have no control over evolution so don't try to control what you cannot. Instead, remain a step ahead at all times so she is aware of the changes as they happen and know she can discuss them with you. Child abuse is another topic you should be discussing at this age. By no means do you need to go into detailed discussions as you can decide how far you talk about these things depending on your daughter's emotional growth. Some girls may start being inquisitive about their bodies by the age of nine, and some later at the age of 12 only. Bear in mind that the point she starts wondering what all her body parts do is the point that discussions should be taking place—if you haven't already opened this door of communication.

When having these discussions, trust your instinct. If your daughter gets upset about certain topics, then pause. Perhaps she's not ready for that so don't force it on her if she's not ready to talk about it yet. If she's interested in what you're talking about, then she's ready. Many parents don't like talking about names for body parts, what actually happens during sexual intercourse or how a baby is created. There's a good chance if you haven't taught her these things, she's already learned them from her friends. The earlier you can introduce even the basics of sex, love and intimacy, the easier it will make this an open discussion. Don't feel as though a question your daughter has is disgusting or inappropriate. Allow her to use you as her soundboard.

When it comes to discussing puberty, menstruation and all the changes that are going to happen in her body, this is a conversation you can start when you feel either your daughter or some of her friends are about to head into puberty. Find a book or video that talks about the changing estrogen in her body and how boys differ with their increasing testosterone. It's equally important she learns about the opposite sex. Bring this conversation up when necessary and revisit it constantly as she moves through puberty. In these early years, it's about affirming that what is happening in her body and what she thinks and feels is normal.

During these early tween years is when discussions about sexism and sexualization should also start happening. These are conversations that aren't always positive but need to be addressed, and it's better the knowledge comes from you rather than elsewhere. As soon as your daughter hears something enough that she believes it's "normal," it can have a lasting consequence. If she's constantly bombarded with the fact that females need to look good, she will naturally focus on it above her thinking abilities. The way you verbally and non-verbally address other women, and men is the best way you can teach her that everyone is different and there is no "one-size-fits-all" when it comes to people's looks or personalities.

Given social media and advertising are in your daughter's face from an early age, the sexualization these images have can negatively detriment her thoughts on sexual and behavioral appeal. She may sexually objectify herself without understanding the error in her actions. This act alone impairs your daughter's cognitive and emotional consequences, mental and physical health, and sexual development. As a parent, if your outer appearance is of high value to you, you've likely passed this mindset to your daughter. Owning up to it and apologizing to her would be a healthy start. The best way to avoid sexualization is to encourage her abilities on the inside. Her activities, her academic prowess, and overall confidence have nothing to do with beauty.

Depending on the development of your daughter, on average, around the age of 12 or 13, she will start questioning her gender disposition and how she is romantically and sexually attracted to other people, both male and female. It may also be the age when inadequate feelings of gender identity come about and teenagers may have an increased inner feeling of being more male or female, or both. When your daughter tells you one day, "Mom, please don't be angry, but I think I might be gay as I like boys and girls," don't have a heart attack. Many (not all) parents accept a boy or girl being gay but hearing it out of the mouth of a 12-year-old can be a little unexpected. Life today isn't the same as twenty years ago and in all honesty, we need to respect the era in which our children grow up and the freedom they have in being open about their sexual choices.

Your daughter's home needs to be a safe environment where she is not judged but accepted. Talking about genders is imperative as during this age it's not as simple as it once was because people talk about being gay (attracted to the same sex), bisexual (attracted to both sexes), demisexual (have sexual intimacy only after an emotional bond is formed), or pansexual (interested in having relationships with all genders). If you suspect your daughter might not feel natural in her body, brush up on the terminology and get your gender vernaculars correct. Gender identity and sexual orientation are not mirrors of each other. Sexual orientation is who your daughter is romantically or sexually attracted to. Gender identity is her innermost concept of self. Whether that be female, male, or a bit of both. It's how she perceives herself. Like much of your role as a parent, being the role model goes way above and beyond everything else. When you hear about a person or you both see someone that is talking about genders on television, talk about how much you think it's great that all people and genders are respected. This doesn't encourage your daughter to be what she isn't, but it does encourage her firstly, to know that you're open to the discussion and two, that she needs to not judge other people on their differences either.

Especially in these teen years, many children that fall into the trans or non-binary categories face a high risk of violence and ostracization from other people their own age. There are both positive and negative peer pressures. Some children may be punished for gender-non-compliant behavior or rewarded for behaving in a socially acceptable manner. We should never push our daughter to confirm a gender due to our own feelings and emotions on the matter. When you put down your daughter's sexual choices, it hurts more than anyone on the outside doing the same.

So, if your daughter does say she likes men and women in her teenage years, it doesn't dictate that when she's older she will have any sexual orientation other than "straight." She is exploring, and that is perfectly okay. What she needs to hear from you is that you're open to her—as you love her right now for who she is. No matter who she is and who she chooses to be, she is perfect to you.

I find myself feeling rather emotional when I talk about genders and acceptance from parents. When I was ten, I remember my youngest uncle who was twenty at the time—my favorite uncle of all—told his parents that he was gay. His mother accepted him fully and respected his choice. His father shunned him and pushed him away and failed to accept him for who he was. He went through his 20s feeling ostracized. There was so much he didn't understand about himself and who he was, and he never had a safety net at home either. Throughout his twenties, he went from one failed gay relationship to the next. Around the age of 30, my uncle was diagnosed with HIV/Aids. Several years later he died, still ignored by his own father. Several years after that my grandfather fell terminally ill with brain cancer and died too. I often wonder if he died with the regret of never forgiving his son over his sexual orientation. And that for me is the hardest thing to accept as a mother. Tomorrow is never promised to any of us. I would never want to lose my girls due to them being different from me physically, mentally, sexually, or morally.

Gender roles, stereotypes, and sexualization all begin early as unwittingly and we as parents can perpetuate them. Did you dress your baby girl in frills, lace, and various shades of pink? You probably didn't question yourself when you did. And don't get me wrong, the media and manufacturers are at fault too as they supply the coolest outfits in those colors! The best we can do as parents, from a young age, is to encourage our daughter to pursue her own interests whether it be doll playing, karate, or video games. It's about finding her own identity that is not biased by our choices. Teaching your daughter to have acceptance of herself, or friends and family, and for LGBTQ identities, encourages her to be a positive force in our ongoing world in accepting all people—regardless of how diversified. Remind yourself, and her, that no matter what gender a person goes to bed with, it doesn't change who they are as a person or their capabilities in the workforce for what they one day become.

Question:

What aspect in this chapter helps you address your biggest fears when it comes to your daughter understanding love and who she is?

1. That she'll be influenced into pornography.
2. That she's feeling unsure about her sexual preferences, and you fear where that could lead.
3. That she may have sex.

6

GOOD DAYS AHEAD

From the moment your daughter is born, she's in your life forever. When she reaches 18 you may breathe a sigh of relief and consider cracking open a bottle of bubbly. However, even though her teenage years are almost over; your days of parenting are not. Your supportive, nurturing, understanding and loving attributes are still required so I suggest you leave the bubbly chilling in the fridge for a while longer. As your daughter nears the end of her schooling days, the next step is making decisions about what to do with her life. Will she head straight into the workforce, does she envision traveling, going to college, or is the idea of hanging out on your couch and getting her clothes washed for a while longer too appealing?

The more your daughter has grasped decision-making skills in her teens, the better she'll be able to make good choices for what to do with her life after school. The more you can help her strengthen these skills, the better. Perhaps she has a particular feeling about a topic and it's bothering her. Maybe she's trying to decide between two career choices or which friend's party to attend that fall on the same day. In an effort for her to make her own decisions you can ask her questions like:

1. What exactly is it that you're feeling right now? What emotion?
2. If there are a few emotions, which is the strongest and which is the weakest?
3. When did you start feeling this way?

Once she's established the feelings, she needs to start gaining some facts before a decision can be made. These might be:

1. What problem is she trying to solve?
2. In solving the problem, what is she trying to achieve? (Such as keeping both friends happy.)
3. What is the best outcome she hopes to get out of this decision and the worst outcome?

Even as adults we often see only the problem directly in front of us and nothing else. Encouraging your daughter to write down multiple solutions and options is a terrific way for her to understand there is always more than one possible outcome. Each solution will come with its own set of positives and negatives. Suggest to her to consider long-term and short-term outcomes depending on the question at hand. Perhaps she's considering dropping out of school. In this manner, she needs to think about the short-term and long-term consequences of her actions. Don't forget to praise your daughter on her decision-making process especially given decisions are not easy for them to make in these unstable years. Ask her to reflect on her decision later. Does she think she made the right decision? If she could go back and make the decision again, would it differ?

Parents should never instill that there is a need for their children to go to college after school. It isn't for everyone. It takes people of all strengths, weaknesses, and interests for this world to work together. It's about finding an environment and opportunity that she feels she fits into. If she isn't wired academically, don't set her up for possible failure. Don't make her feel like anything less than the awesome young woman she is because she doesn't want to go to college.

Sit down with her regularly and go over all the pros and cons she has about these decisions. Remind her that not getting into a college she desires or getting a job with the first interview she attends are the same for everyone. Effort always outweighs anything else. Your only goal as the parent during this time is to liberate her from feeling as though she needs to mimic someone else to be successful.

Many teens are so exhausted after their schooling years that they want time out. And this can be beneficial for some. Perhaps your daughter may want to travel or do community service. If she is interested in traveling, encourage her to get a part-time job while she's still at school to begin saving up. If you do have some finances to support in a minor way in her travels or taking time off, discuss this with her. She should never assume you can afford what she has in her head. Set limits so that she understands you are supporting as much as you can, but more than that you cannot offer.

Perhaps she wants to go straight into the working world as she feels uncertain about the future. Whether that be in the form of a gap year to give her time to decide, or she's made the decision that college is not for her. Gap years are excellent if she works within that year. Experiencing life and taking direction from managers will offer her life skills and emotional intelligence. If she does decide to go to college after that year, chances are she'll be ahead of other students, and she learned a great deal of commitment and discipline skills in that year that will benefit her in college. Getting a job means teaching her about searching for employment, developing interview skills, and writing a resume. Depending on her area of interest, there are many companies out there that will contract an employee on a lower salary and contribute to further educational studies that relate to their employment. This is a terrific way of learning practically and academically at the same time.

Likely, for your daughter to consider her future is a little too much to handle and it's the last thing she wants to do in her final school years. But at some point, the ball needs to start rolling. This is not the time in her life for you to make decisions. This is her time. Like every aspect in her life, listen to her. Chances are she knows she needs to figure out what to do with the rest of her life, but it's a scary and daunting prospect. Support her in the fact that you understand completely how hard it is to make those kinds of choices.

What helps during these hard decisions is if you already have in place within your home a way of teaching her the skills to make her own choices as well as mastering day-to-day living skills. By her late teens, she should already be capable of doing grocery shopping, cooking basic meals, cleaning the house, and understanding how to budget money. The best way for teens to learn this is to have clear set chores that need to be done within the household on a regular basis. You cannot let these chores lapse and consistency is key. One day when she lives on her own, she also can't not pay her bills simply because she doesn't feel like it.

When your daughter starts ruminating on her decisions later in life, it's normal for her to feel lost. She's always had you, her teachers, friends, or coaches helping and directing her and suddenly, it's entirely up to her. Don't make her feel alone in the void of decision and help her. For example, perhaps she's considering an internship to see if she likes a specific field of interest. Browse the internet with her and make note of some workplaces she feels she'd like to get in contact with.

If your daughter is interested in going to college after school, things are a little different from when you finished your schooling years. Many teenagers need to start this process early due to the extensive research involved along with deadlines for applications and competition to get in. What she wants to do with her life is up to her but that doesn't mean you cannot be there for her to bounce ideas off. Sometimes school-teachers or guidance counselors in schools can be a great help. Often parents have an outdated view of colleges, the courses offered, and what happens after that—given job perspectives have evolved so much. Even the aspect of game designing is not simple and diverse with different areas of development. If she is considering studying but feeling unsure about what course to take, encourage her to write down goals and accomplishments. She can be proactive and write about her strengths and weaknesses, what brings her joy and where she had the most successful grades during school. She also needs to consider in this written list where her college choices are. Does she want to study close to home, far afield or do online studies?

The path to making decisions after school isn't always obvious and tell her that for many this may take years to figure out. Let your daughter know she does need to take her thoughts and research seriously. That's why exploring various options is helpful. Anxiety and stress can run high in these later high school years so ease the burden and help her become more apt at utilizing her alarm clock to take charge of her time and her calendar to set up activities and schedules. A great way to improve her life skills is by giving her more responsibility.

If your daughter is taking medication, you need to start thinking about how she'll manage this herself when she moves out from under your roof. Encourage and teach her to monitor herself, how she's feeling, and being responsible for her health. So as the parent, utilize these last years to empower teenagers to be self-reliant rather than codependent. Failure is a normal part of life as well as dealing with challenges. Often, the best way of talking to your daughter is drawing from your own experiences at that time in your life to provide support.

It's also not unfamiliar when thinking about career choices for your daughter to only tell you half their story. There could be many reasons for this and likely, they don't want to be judged by you for their career choices, or they're telling themselves they've got this, and they can figure it out. She'll tell you the side of the story, and her future, that she wants you to hear. She doesn't mean to withhold anything from you. She loves you and doesn't want to hurt you, especially if her choices vary greatly from what you may have expressed is your own. Make sure your daughter has other trusted adults and mentors she can turn to apart from parents. Let her know that if she cannot tell all the gory details to you, she needs to know she can turn to them. And don't feel hurt in the process.

Once, you gave her roots. Now, you're giving her wings.

Before you know it, she'll be out of her self-proclaimed hotel you call home. You'll no longer be bossed around by a teenager who believes you're too old to understand the world and only her, and her peers understand the true essence of what life is about. Despite the drama and gray hairs, her teenage years have given you. Watching her fly is a momentous and wonderful thing and you've successfully undergone the hardest and most important job you'll ever do in your life. Parenting. Now is the time to open that bottle of bubbly and congratulate yourself on helping your daughter take the first momentous steps into the world on her own.

For many of us, this feeling of celebration is tinged with a deep sadness. It's like working your whole life, dedicating yourself to a job title, and suddenly, you're retrenched. But there is no reason to let empty feelings set in as you know she will always need your advice and always need to find solace under the roof of your home. You marveled when she was a toddler, or when she went to her first day of school and had her first day in high school. It was a big deal. Finishing school is a moment for you to cherish as well.

LEAVE A 1-CLICK REVIEW!

Customer Reviews

★★★★★ 2
5.0 out of 5 stars ▾

5 star	▬▬▬▬▬▬▬	100%
4 star		0%
3 star		0%
2 star		0%
1 star		0%

See all verified purchase reviews ›

Share your thoughts with other customers

Write a customer review

I would be incredible thankful if you could take just 60 seconds to write a brief review on Amazon, even if it's just a few sentences!

CONCLUSION

Consider the teenage years an epic voyage across open seas. A voyage is a journey from one point to another. It involves discovery in unveiling the unknown and unfathomable. There are times your daughter may have been holed up in her cabin with her back braced against the wall as steely gray clouds, wind and lightning ravaged the ocean. With each heave and roll, her stomach churned. There are times she may have looked out at an expanse of beauty and wonder as the sun glistened across the water's surface and whales breached. Or perhaps she felt out of her depth when the ocean resembled a desert as the sun beat down so fiercely, with not a drop of fresh water in sight.

The itinerary is alluring.

Do you long for escape? Do you want to start taking control and put life in your own hands?

Well, jump on board.

We offer you danger, adventure, and the perilous undertakings of investigating the deepest parts of yourself.

A journey engrossed in wonderment; it will unveil all your heart desires.

You'll seek treasures, take gratifying risks, and discover the marvels found deep in your psyche.

Line up and get your tickets right here.

The voyage departs every month of every year, so don't miss out on this once-in-a-lifetime opportunity!

Sounds rather like one of those advertisements that offer the world and beyond, doesn't it? If other teenagers are buying into it, shouldn't your daughter too?

A few things are required for a ship to make a successful journey across the seas. A Captain is required to lead the way. A First Mate is also necessary because let's face it, you may become redundant before your time. And then a compass. It might not always be reliable, but it still serves a purpose of general guidance. Go for it, you can take the role as Captain and be the moral compass for your daughter, the First Mate. In the early days of this voyage, you'll realize your value as Captain lies in listening, not commanding.

Parenting teenage daughters isn't necessarily harder than parenting young girls. It really isn't. However, if you go into your daughter's teenage years with the mentality that you can approach it in the same way, you'll falter. Your role as a parent needs to shift. Don't feel undermined but empowered that your daughter is growing and thriving, and you no longer need to be her primary decision-maker. In addition to "stepping down" in your role as Captain, remember that we live in the 21st century. Whatever teenagers want to find out about sex, love, drugs and rock n' roll, there's no substitute for the internet. They are much more advanced at utilizing it than you are. It may even empower them that they know so much more than you. I say yes, my daughters do know more about me in many instances, but not in life experience. I'm afraid that all the notches in the years I have on them still put me out in front. So, take on this new role in parenting like the Captain of the ship. Allow your First Mate to learn everything you know and although much of that understanding will only come over time and with experience, if your daughter has the tools, she'll be able to navigate on her own soon enough.

We're all human and there are times that we as parents have a great deal to say. What can start as a casual conversation can easily turn into an emotional minefield. No one ever said parenting was easy and I'm quite sure you've figured that out already as the years leading up to your daughter becoming a teenager haven't been a breeze either. One day, you'll be sailing your ship into the most magnificent horizon the world has to offer. You need to know that when you do so, she'll be able to make it on her own in this vast ocean of life. Being mindful is truly my favorite go-to word. Relax. Accept your new role, and you, and your daughter, are going to be just fine!

It feels like only yesterday when my daughters were 11 and would come with me to the pet store regularly to buy all we needed for the animals. I specifically remember once as we pulled the car up to the home and the radio was playing the song "Sandy" to the *Grease* movie. We all loved it and had watched *Grease* together many times before. I switched the car off, turned the radio volume up and let the song keep playing. The three of us sang at the top of our lungs until the song ended. I remember that moment. I walked into the house with them bouncing off ahead of me and I smiled. It was as though I said goodbye to my little girls in that instant. And that's how quickly it can happen. One moment they are your little girls, and the next, they're something different. We've been on that epic voyage. We survived the tumultuous seas, braced ourselves through the storms we never thought we'd see the end of, and held each other's hands as the beauty of life beckoned. And we survived; together.

What I have now, today, I wouldn't give up for the world!

The journey I underwent with my daughters was personal and, in this book, I hope to empower you and make your journey a little easier. I can't undertake this voyage on behalf of you or your daughter, as every journey is different. However, I can help you to read the stars. If I had learned a little more about using the stars to navigate rather than my unreliable compass before I set sail, I possibly wouldn't have made so many failed passages.

To be frank, teenage years are unfortunately not an advertisement offering the world and you can choose buying into or not. You failed to read the fine print when you gave birth that you have already made the purchase. Is it easy raising teenagers? No. Is it easy to keep your cool when none of your daughter's emotional outbursts make any sense? No. Yet you get through it with joy, just as you did when she was learning to sit, crawl, walk, her troublesome toddler years and beyond. She held your hand for dear life through it all.

Breathe.

Enjoy the many days the voyage offers of tranquil oceans. In those times, together, you can delve into the wonders of imagining, thinking, and learning. Teenagers have traversed these vast waters for generations. The ships may have changed, as have the navigating tools. And your First Mate no longer needs or wants to hold your hand. She wants something more than that. She wants to stand by your side.

Whether your daughter is heading into her teen years or is already in the midst of them, take time to figure out what are the most important factors for you and utilize the tools I've offered to set yourself up with some ways of tackling them. It's never too late to make changes.

In this book, I've offered you some hope that your little girl isn't lost, and you need to be there more for her than ever before. If you have a friend or family member who has a daughter, please share this book with them. And don't forget to leave a review if this book has helped you.

A SPECIAL GIFT TO OUR READERS

Included with your purchase of this book is our *"4 Ways to spend Quality time with your teenage daughter"*.

This checklist will provide you ways to re-connect with your daughter.

Go to the link below and let us know which email address to deliver it to:

www.TammyCobbs.com

REFERENCES

(Mossakowski, K. (2003). Coping with Perceived Discrimination: Does Ethnic Identity Protect Mental Health? Journal of Health and Social Behavior, 44(3), 318-331. doi:10.2307/1519782).

(Jones, Jason D.; Ehrlich, Katherine B.; Lejuez, C. W.; Cassidy, Jude. "Parental knowledge of adolescent activities: Links with parental attachment style and adolescent substance use." Journal of Family Psychology, Vol 29(2), Apr 2015, 191-200. http://dx.doi.org/10. 1037/fam0000070).

Olweus, D. (1993). Bullying at school: What we know and What we can do. Boston, MA: Blackwell.

Copeland, W.E., Wolke, D., Angold, A., and Costello E.J., (2013). Adult psychiatric outcomes of bullying and been bullied by peers in childhood and adolescence. JAMA Psychiatry 70 (4) 419-26; Teicher, M. H., Samsom, J. A., Shew, Y., et al. (2010). Hurtful words: Exposure to peer verbal aggression is associated with elevated psychiatric symptom scores and corpus callosum abnormalities. American Journal of Psychiatry 167 (12), 1464-71.

https://pediatrics.aappublications.org/content/140/4/e20163494.

https://www.ncbi.nlm.nih.gov/pmc/articles/PMC3705203/).

Salmivalli, C., Voeten, M., & Poskiparta, E. (2011). Bystanders matter: Associations between reinforcing, defending, and the frequency of bullying behavior in classrooms. Journal of Clinical Child & Adolescent Psychology, 40 (5), 668-676.

Merrel, K.W., Buchanan, R. Tram. O.K., 2006. Relational aggression in children and adolescents: A review with implications for school settings. Psychology in the Schools 43 (3), 345-60, p.348.

Misra S, Cheng L, Genevie J, Yuan M. The iPhone Effect: The Quality of In-Person Social Interactions in the Presence of Mobile Devices. Environment and Behavior. 2016;48(2):275-298. doi:10.1177/0013916514539755.

Rath. T., "Are You Fully Charged?" 2015. Silicon Guild; Illustrated edition (May 15, 2015).

(https://www.sciencedirect.com/science/article/abs/pii/S0959438807000414).

Kelly McGonigal., "The willpower instinct" Avery Trade; edition 2013.

Boyd., Danah., It's Complicated - The Social Lives of Networked Teens, Yale University Press | 2014, https://doi.org/10.12987/9780300166439.

https://www.edweek.org/leadership/should-schools-be-giving-so-many-failing-grades-this-year/2020/12).

Johnson. Ned., "The Self-Driven Child" Penguin Books; 2019.

Deci. Edward L., "Why We Do What We Do" Penguin Books; edition 1996.

Lyubomirsky. Sonja., "The Myths of Happiness", Penguin Books 2014.

(https://mottpoll.org/reports/how-pandemic-has-impacted-teen-mental-health?utm_source=STAT+Newsletters&utm_campaign=dd0df333b3-MR_COPY_14&utm_medium=email&utm_term=0_8cab1d7961-dd0df333b3-149698521.

(Costello, E.J., Mustillo, S., Erkanli, A., et al. 2003. Prevalence and development of psychiatric disorders in childhood and adolescence. Archives of General Psychiatry 60 (8), 837-44.

6th ed. Sifton, E. (2003). The serenity prayer: Faith and politics in times of peace and war. New York: Norton.

Moisala, M., Salmela, V., Salo, E., Carlson, S., Vuontela, V., Salonen, O., & Alho, K. (2015). Brain activity during divided and selective attention to auditory and visual sentence comprehension tasks. Frontiers in human neuroscience, 9, 86. https://doi.org/10.3389/fnhum.2015.00086.

Richard Davidson PhD, Sharon Begley., "The Emotional Life of Your Brain - How Its Unique Patterns Affect the Way You Think, Feel, and Live - and How You Can Change Them", Hudson Street Press; 1st edition (March 1, 2012).

Thapar. A., Collishaw, S., Pine, D.S., Tapara's., 2012. Depression in adolescence. Lancet 379 (9820), I056-67.

Essau, C.A., & Chang, W. C. (2009). Epidemiology, comorbidity, and course of adolescent depression. In C. A. Essau (Ed.), Treatments for adolescent depression: Theory and practice. (pp. 3-26). Oxford, NY. Oxford University Press.).

Hankin, B. L., Wetter, E., & Cheely, C. (2008). Sex differences in child and adolescent depression: A developmental psychopathological approach. In J. R. Z. Abella & B. L. Hankin (Eds.), Handbook of depression in children and adolescents (pp. 377-415). New York, NY: Guilford Press.).

O'Keefe, G. S., Clarke-Pearson, K., & Council on Communications and Media. (2011). Clinical report – the impact of social media on children, adolescents, and families. Pediatrics: Official Journal of the American Academy of Pediatrics, 127, 800-804. doi:10.1542/peds.2011-0054.

Dweck, Carol. "Mindset The New Psychology of Success," Random House; Illustrated edition. 2006.

Lyubomirsky, Sonja. The how of happiness: A scientific approach to getting the life you want. Penguin Books; Illustrated edition (Dec 30, 2008).

Jacka FN, Kremer PJ, Leslie ER, et al. Associations Between Diet Quality and Depressed Mood in Adolescents: Results from the Australian Healthy Neighbourhoods Study. Australian & New Zealand Journal of Psychiatry. 2010;44(5):435-442. doi:10.3109/00048670903571598).

Ratey, John J M.D. "Spark: The Revolutionary New Science of Exercise and the Brain". Little, Brown Spark; Reprint edition (Jan. 1, 2013).

Cuddy, Amy. "Presence". Little, Brown Spark; Large type / Large print edition (Dec 29, 2015).

https://www.ncbi.nlm.nih.gov/pmc/articles/PMC3705203/).

Shroff, H., Thompson, J.K., (2006). Peer influences, body-image dissatisfaction, eating dysfunction and self-esteem in adolescent girls. Journal of Health Psychology II (4), 533-5I.

https://wellbeings.org/events/teens-covid-and-coping/.

(https://www.cdc.gov/alcohol/fact-sheets/underage-drinking.htm.

Blum, R. W., Beuhring, T., Shew, M.L., et al, (2000). The effects of race/ethnicity, income, and family structure on adolescent risk behaviors. American Journal of Public Health 90(I2), 1897-84.

Osgood, D.W., Ragan, D.T., Wallace, L., et al, (2013). Peers and the emergence of alcohol use: Influence and selection processes in adolescent friendship networks. Journal of Research on Adolescence 23 (3), 500-512.

Medina, K.L., McQueeny, T., Nagel, B.J., Hanson, K.L., Schweinsburg, A.D. and Tapert, S.F. (2008), Prefrontal Cortex Volumes in Adolescents With Alcohol Use Disorders: Unique Gender Effects. Alcoholism: Clinical and Experimental Research, 32: 386-394. https://doi.org/10.1111/j.1530-0277.2007.00602.x.

Jacobus, J., Bava, S., Cohen-Zihon, M., et al, (2009). Functional consequences of marijuana use in adolescents. Pharmacology Biochemistry and Behavior 92 (4), 559-65.

Paul, A.B.M., Simms, L., Amini, S. and Paul, A.E. (2018), Teens and Spice: A Review of Adolescent Fatalities Associated with Synthetic Cannabinoid Use. J Forensic Sci, 63: 1321-1324. https://doi.org/10.1111/1556-4029.13704.

https://www.cdc.gov/tobacco/data_statistics/fact_sheets/youth_data/tobacco_use/index.htm).

Lamborn, S.D., Mounts, N.S., Steinberg, L., Dornbush, S.M., (1991). Patterns of competence and adjustment among adolescents from authoritative, authoritarian, indulgent, and neglectful families. Child development 62 (5), 1049-65.

Steinberg, L., Albert, D., Cauffman, E., et al. (2008). Age differences in sensation seeking and impulsivity as indexed by behavior and self-report: Evidence for a dual systems model. Developmental Psychology 44(6), 1764-78.

Steinberg, L., (2001). We know some things: Adolescent-parent relationships in retrospect and prospect. Journal of research on Adolescence 11 (1), 1-19.

Burke, J.D., Hipwell, A.E., and Loeber, R., (2010). Dimensions of oppositional defiant disorder as predictors of depression and conduct disorder in preadolescent girls. Journal of the American Academy of Child and Adolescent Psychiatry 49(5), 484-92.

Zahn-Waxler, C., Crick, N. R., Shirtcliff, E. A., & Woods, K. E. (2006). The origins and development of psychopathology in females and males. In D. Cicchetti & D. J. Cohen (Eds.), Developmental psychopathology: Theory and method (pp. 76–138). John Wiley & Sons, Inc.).

Pietromonaco, P. R., & Overall, N. C. (2021). Applying relationship science to evaluate how the COVID-19 pandemic may impact couples' relationships. American Psychologist, 76(3), 438-450. http://dx.doi.org/10.1037/amp0000714.

Zurbriggen, E.L., Collins, R.L., Lamb, S., ET AL. (2007). Report on the APA Taskforce on the sexualization of Girls, Executive Summary. Washington, DC: American Psychology Association.

(https://www.researchgate.net/
publication/7534515_Exposure_to_Internet_Pornogra
phy_among_Children_and_Adolescents_A_National_
Survey.

Sexual orientation is how you are attracted romantically and sexually to other people -
https://www.healthlinkbc.ca/health-topics/te7288.

Westein, N., Ryan, W.S., DeHann, C.R., et al. (2012).
Parental autonomy support and discrepancies between
implicit and explicit sexual identities: Dynamics of self-
acceptance and defense. Journal of Personality and
Social Psychology 102 (4,815-32.

Ryan, C., Russell, S.T., Huebner, D., et al. (2010). Family
acceptance in adolesce and the health of LGBTQ young
adults. Journal of Child and Adolescent Psychiatric
Nursing 23(4), 205-13.

Bay-Cheng, L.Y., and Fava, N.M., (2011). Young
women's experiences and perceptions of cunnilingus
during adolesce. Journal of Sex Research 48(6), 531-42.

Brady, S.S., Herper-Felsher, B.L., (2007). Adolescents'
reported consequences of having oral sex versus
vaginal sex. Pediatrics 119 (2), 229-36.

Lythcott-Haims, Julie., "How to raise an adult". Henry
Holt and Co.; 0 edition (2015).

https://files.eric.ed.gov/fulltext/EJ1087715.pdf.

https://raisingchildren.net.au/pre-teens/development/understanding-your-pre-teen/pre-teen-development.

https://www.braindirector.com/how-teen-girls-try-to-fit-in-the-modern-society/.

https://www.psychologytoday.com/us/blog/surviving-your-childs-adolescence/201701/social-challenges-middle-school.

https://www.noisolation.com/research/consequences-of-social-isolation-for-children-and-adolescents/.

https://www.apa.org/topics/child-development/stress.

https://mentalhealthliteracy.org/understanding-stress/.

https://www.internationalschoolparent.com/articles/helicopter-parenting-the-consequences/.

https://www.competitionsciences.org/2017/12/07/challenge-vs-threat-mindset-how-to-empower-yourself-and-your-students-to-rise-to-the-challenge/.

https://www.mentalhelp.net/blogs/investigating-the-complicated-emotional-life-of-adolescents/.

https://mindfullifetoday.com/challenge-your-stress-response/.

https://www.psychologytoday.com/us/blog/more-women-s-work/201805/10-rules-living-teenage-daughter.

https://www.bodyshotperformance.com/how-to-move-from-a-threat-mindset-to-a-challenge-mindset-with-martin-johnson/.

https://www.ncbi.nlm.nih.gov/pmc/articles/PMC3677799/.

https://www.teenfocus.org/.

https://www.logosschool.org/about/news/blog/post-details/~board/articles/post/the-importance-of-plan-ning-for-life-after-high-school.

https://grownandflown.com/college-decision-teen-needs-your-help/.

https://www.parents.com/parenting/better-parenting/teenagers/teen-talk/how-teens-decide-what-they-want-to-do-when-they-grow-up/.

https://www.shepherdsfriendly.co.uk/resources/how-to-handle-when-your-first-child-moves-out/.

https://www.sparktheirfuture.qld.edu.au/how-to-help-your-teen-make-good-decisions-about-school-and-life/.

https://www.theguardian.com/education/2013/sep/18/parents-coping-when-children-leave-home.

https://www.relate.org.uk/relationship-help/help-family-life-and-parenting/parenting-teenagers.

https://www.relate.org.uk/.

https://www.psychologytoday.com/us/blog/more-women-s-work/201805/10-rules-living-teenage-daughter.

https://greatergood.berkeley.edu/article/item/three_ways_to_change_your_parenting_in_the_teenage_years.

https://gaycenter.org/about/lgbtq/.

https://www.healthychildren.org/English/ages-stages/gradeschool/puberty/Pages/Talking-to-Your-Child-About-Sex.aspx.

https://www.verywellfamily.com/sexualization-3288347.

https://www.todaysparent.com/family/parenting/how-to-talk-to-kids-about-gender-age-by-age-guide/.

https://www.chop.edu/news/health-tip/talking-to-kids-about-gender-and-sexual-orientation.

https://kidshealth.org/en/kids/about-love.html.

https://kidshealth.org/en/kids/about-love.html.

https://youaremom.com/prevent-your-teenager-from-drinking-alcohol/.

https://youaremom.com/children/teenage-girls-fall-in-love/.

https://www.focusonthefamily.com/parenting/how-pornography-affects-a-teen-brain/.

https://www.havenwoodacademy.org/four-modern-issues-pornography-has-created-for-teen-girls/.

https://childmind.org/article/talking-to-your-kids-about-porn/.

https://www.goodtherapy.org/blog/parent-teen-relations-affect-intimacy-later-in-life-021014.

https://www.healthyfamiliesbc.ca/home/articles/guide-teenagers-and-alcohol.

https://paradigmtreatment.com/top-six-teen-risk-behaviors/.

https://www.heysigmund.com/teenagers-and-risky-behaviour/.

https://www.focusonthefamily.ca/content/how-to-heal-the-damage-caused-by-parent-teen-conflict.

https://parenthetical.wisc.edu/2017/11/06/breaking-the-cycle-8-strategies-for-dealing-with-conflict-with-your-young-teen/.

https://somaticmovementcenter.com/challenge-threat-stress-response/.

https://myactivity.google.com/activitycontrols/webandapp.

https://www.verywellmind.com/what-to-do-if-you-think-your-child-has-an-eating-disorder-4062806.

https://www.betterhealth.vic.gov.au/health/healthyliving/teenagers-and-sleep.

https://bouncebackparenting.com/6-methods-to-inspire-your-teen-to-get-exercise/.

https://yourteenmag.com/family-life/communication/helicopter-parents-2.

https://www.healthline.com/health/understanding-tweens-a-transformative-age.

https://everfi.com/blog/community-engagement/mental-health-social-distancing-young-adults/.

https://mentalhealthliteracy.org/product/parenting-your-teen/.

https://www.aacap.org/AACAP/Families_and_Youth/Facts_for_Families/FFF-Guide/Helping-Teenagers-With-Stress-066.aspx.

https://www.apa.org/topics/child-development/stress.

https://raisingchildren.net.au/teens/behaviour/peers-friends-trends/tattoos-piercings.

https://www.empoweringparents.com/article/does-your-child-have-toxic-friends-6-ways-to-deal-with-the-wrong-crowd/.

https://yourteenmag.com/social-life/teenagers-friends/making-bad-decisions.

https://trailscarolina.com/blog/teen-social-isolation-dangers-alone/.

https://www.verywellfamily.com/reasons-why-teens-bully-others-460532.

https://www.surreysfamilyhelphub.org.uk/teenagers/bullying.

https://www.psychologytoday.com/us/blog/surviving-your-childs-adolescence/201701/social-challenges-middle-school.

https://yourteenmag.com/social-life/teenagers-friends/teens-talk-about-popularity.

https://www.familyeducation.com/life/cliques/cliques-fitting.

https://www.apa.org/pi/families/resources/adolescent-girls.

https://www.psychologytoday.com/us/blog/special-matters/201905/how-parent-the-teen-struggle-fit-in-and-stand-out.

https://www.braindirector.com/how-teen-girls-try-to-fit-in-the-modern-society/.

https://howtoparentateen.wordpress.com/2012/02/21/teenage-girls-friends/.

https://raisingchildren.net.au/pre-teens/family-life.